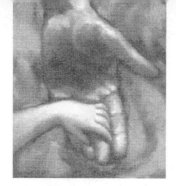

PASSING

ON

THE

Prayer Legacy

THE EARNEST PRAYER OF A RIGHTEOUS [PARENT] HAS GREAT POWER AND
WONDERFUL RESULTS

_____

(Name of Child)

_____

(Date)

My child, these are the people who have prayed for you, asking God to help
shape you into a person who is just like Him.

_____   _____

_____   _____

_____   _____

_____   _____

_____   _____

Prayer Legacy

As you use this book, think of it not only as a prayer journal that you will read over in the coming months and years but also as a keepsake prayer journal that you will pass on to your child as a witness to God's involvement in his or her life over a period of time. As you record your prayers, God's responses, and your reflections about the growth of God's character in your child, you are recording a legacy.

This book becomes an altar, a memorial like the one Joshua had the people erect when they crossed the Jordan River into the Promised Land (Josh. 4). The Israelites built a memorial of stones so that whenever a family passed by the stones and the children would ask, "What do these stones mean?" the parents could tell the story of God's faithfulness in bringing them through the wilderness.

In this keepsake prayer journal, you do two things: You lay your requests on the altar, submitting them to God's mercy; and you erect a memorial to God's faithfulness in your child's life, so that when your child asks at a later time, "What do these prayers mean?" you can share the story of how God revealed His character in and through your child's life.

May the Lord who blesses children bless you as you erect this memorial to His glory.

LORD, BLESS MY CHILD

LORD BLESS MY CHILD

WILLIAM & NANCIE CARMICHAEL

 TYNDALE HOUSE PUBLISHERS, INC. WHEATON, ILLINOIS

ISBN 0-8423-2047-4

Printed in the United States of America

00 99 98 97 96 95
 7   6   5   4   3   2   1

We dedicate this book to our children:
May you be like cities set on a hill,
lights that cannot be hidden.

CONTENTS

Part 3, LORD, BLESS MY CHILD WITH . . .

Part 4, LORD, HELP MY CHILD TO DESIRE TO . . .

Part 5, LORD, HELP MY CHILD TO BECOME . . .

As I sat on an airplane reading the manuscript for this book, the woman one seat away explained that she is an advertising photographer. She commented extensively on how people are looking for answers and how they are inspired by hopeful pictures like eagles soaring. Then she asked abruptly, "Who is your favorite inspirational author these days?"

I smiled and answered, "As I read this manuscript, it is fast becoming Bill and Nancie Carmichael." Intrigued, she asked if it would be permissible for her to take a peek at the book before it was published. I told her I thought the authors would be delighted for her to know what they had written. I dug out the first chapter and passed it to her.

In the meantime a young man, himself a writer and editor, sat down between us. After the usual get-acquainted chatter about who we are and what I was reviewing, he became intensely interested in the manuscript. As the woman passed each page back to me, he intercepted it and eagerly read it. "I have one young child and another one on the way, and I desperately need to know how to bring them up. Do you think this book could help me?" I assured him it would, and he asked how soon the book would be available so that he could buy one.

Suddenly I had an idea. "I'll give your name to the authors, and they can send you one as soon as it is off the press!" His big smile of relief assured me that he knew this book really is the answer to the frightening task of bringing up children in today's world.

This is not just a book of family prayers for superficial, immediate needs. It is a hands-on manual of instruction, including family interaction, Scripture passages on which to meditate, reverent yet down-to-earth prayers, and lessons to be applied in our lives and in our children's lives. This book shows how our prayers can unlock Christlike attributes in our children—and in us.

This book provides a simple outline to follow, bringing whole families day-by-day into conformity to God's dear Son, Jesus. What a different country we would have if all parents conscientiously worked at producing this lifestyle in their families!

And what a priceless gift this book is to pass on to children and for them to pass on to their children. The prayer journal will chronicle the weekly struggles, answers from God, and spiritual growth. When you pass on your completed journal to your children when they are older—maybe as a high school graduation gift—and when they read what you have written, they will see firsthand the power of God's presence in shaping their lives.

But, as Bill and Nancie point out, godly character traits are caught, not just taught. This profound advice from the depths of their own hearts is the abundant overflow of their own intense journey with God. What they have modeled for their children could and should become the example of what we can become for our children and grandchildren.

The books I have written about prayer are filled with illustrations of our deep family prayers of power, guidance, protection, security, and submission to God's will. These prayers have been the warp and woof of the fabric of our family life for fifty-three years. But I have wept at the thousands of life-sustaining and life-changing prayers I could not include. So I am thrilled that here is a book to *enrich* and *extend* your family's prayer life—and ours.

When this book is produced, I want to be the first to get my copy as a mother and grandmother. Then I want the next three copies for the people dearest to me—my children, who already know so much about the necessity, power, and privilege of prayer—so that they also can have their family prayer lives enriched and extended by this incredible book.

When you finish using this book, you may have the same experience I did. My eyes filled with tears, and my heart cried, "Here truly is one of today's great Christian classics!" May God bless you as you pray, "Lord, bless my child."

Evelyn Christenson

ACKNOWLEDGMENTS

Significant people have helped us with this book. Thank you, Norma Cole and Kathy Boice, for your valuable assistance. Thank you, Lynn Vanderzalm, and the entire staff of Tyndale House Publishers for your dedicated professionalism and your vision for this book. Good friends Steve and Cindy Johnson and Duane and LeeAnn Rawlins, thank you for listening to us dream about this book; you are true encouragers. Earl and Dorothy Book, our spiritual mentors, thank you for showing us the joys of a prayer-filled life.

We're also thankful for the privilege of being associated with the creative and supportive people at *Virtue* and *Christian Parenting Today* and the great family of Cook Communications, Inc.

We are forever grateful to Nancie's parents, Gunder and Harriet Pearson (now in heaven), and to Bill's parents, Harold and Betty Carmichael, who held us in their arms and hearts and who through the years have prayed for us without ceasing. And most of all, we thank our children—the light of our lives—for being the inspiration for this book.

I (Bill) first noticed it when I was in the bedroom I shared with my younger brother in our house on Rutland Avenue in San Jose, California. I was seven years old. The house was small, with only two bedrooms, one bathroom, a tiny kitchen with a formica-topped table, a small living room, and a back porch, where my older sister slept.

The walls of that house were so thin that we could hear almost everything anyone said. As I drifted off to sleep at night, I often heard my parents discussing things in the kitchen or laughing with friends in the living room or talking softly to each other in their bedroom.

But that night, for the first time, I was not just hearing, I was listening. I listened to my father praying: "O God, we love You and want You to be the Lord of our lives. We pray for our chil-dren, dear Lord." As I listened, I heard my name: "And for Billy we pray that You will begin to speak to his heart about following You. We pray that You will give us wisdom in raising this boy. We pray that You will wrap Your loving and protecting arms around him and that Your heav-enly angels will watch over him. . . ."

Somehow I knew I was witness to the sacred. I knew this was the Holy of Holies. I knew I was hearing my father's faith, out of the Sunday ser-vice and into his everyday life. I knew this was real.

As his oldest son, I was profoundly affected by his prayers and faith. I knew from then on that I was under some kind of special protection and direc-tion. My own spiritual significance began to take on meaning for me from that moment.

Praying Fathers

Now, almost forty-five years later, I can still hear my father's wonderful voice in prayer. I have heard it thousands of times, but I never tire of hearing it again. My father is now eighty-three. Just last week he called me and asked where I was going to speak this week and then ended the conversation by saying, "I'll be praying for you." This past summer I took my father on a fishing trip, and just after we turned out the lights, we prayed together. I felt as if I were his small child again as I heard his voice in earnest prayer to God.

After staying overnight at his grandparents' home last year, our oldest son, Jon, called me and said, "Dad, you should hear Grandpa pray at night. He goes down the list of all of his children and grandchildren one by one before going to sleep at night. He prays for each one of us. It was so special to hear him call out my name to God."

"Yes, Jon, I know," I said. "And I am glad you had the chance to hear it for yourself."

My mother also prayed faithfully for me, but I mention my father because it seems as if few fathers in today's world see the incredible importance of praying for their children and grandchildren. I will always cherish my dad's prayers for me as something special.

Like my dad, I have tried to be a praying father. I confess that at times this has been less of a priority than it should have been. At times I have allowed my schedule and business activities to crowd prayer into erratic and inconsistent spurts. But I always come back to the fact that it is the one thing that I am called to do and that I am capable of doing for my children. I know that as grandchildren will inevitably come, my prayer job has only just begun.

When Nancie and I developed the idea for this book, we wanted to make it a helpful tool for all parents and grandparents. But I want it to be especially useful for fathers to focus their prayers for their children in an organized way.

A History of Prayer

Recently my mother gave me the diaries of my aunt Hazel, who died a few years ago. As I was reading her daily entries, most of which simply told of where she had been, whom she had seen, and what she had eaten, I came across an entry dated February 7, 1943: "Harold and Betty had Billy dedicated at church this morning." Once again a simple statement, found in my aunt's diary, confirmed to me my parents' resolve to have God involved in the shaping of my life.

Sometimes I regret that we live in a big house, where our bedroom is not on the same floor as our children's bedrooms. Our children have rarely heard our prayers for them at night. But they do know we pray. We pray for them and with them daily. For years we prayed for the unknown spouse of each of our children. Now we know who one of them is. Our oldest son, Jonathan, married Brittni this past summer.

After the wedding reception, I handed Jonathan a note and said, "Please read this before you go to bed tonight." In that note to Jon and Brittni I wrote,

Dear Jon and Brittni,

I can hardly believe that by the time you read this letter, you will be married and on your way to a great life together. I feel so honored to be your dad, Jon, and honored to be your new "dad-in-law," Brit.

I just want you two to know how proud I am of you both and how much confidence I have in you as a couple. You have a wonderful heritage and a wonderful future.

I want to encourage you from the very beginning to start the habit of praying together as a couple every day. I suggest that you begin this habit tonight, the first night of your honeymoon.

Nancie and I have made this our practice, and I believe it has made all the difference in our relationship and in helping us raise our family.

I know that you love God and have asked Jesus to be your Savior. And I know you know that being His disciples is more than a onetime commitment. But your mom and I know from our own experience that it takes a daily conscious effort to make Him Lord of your family and keep Him on the throne of your hearts.

One thing we commit to do for you

until we die is to continue to pray for you every day, as our parents have done for us.

Love,

Dad and Mom

Taking Note of What We Pray

Several years ago, I began to take note of the specifics of the spontaneous prayers I was praying for our children. To my surprise I found much repetition. I discovered that I prayed most often for their safety and protection, adding a few prayers about an attitude or physical problem. I realized that I could be praying with a much larger agenda.

Often as parents, we feel out of control. We fear that the world's allure, the peer pressure, and the natural wayward bent of the human spirit will take our children far away from God. While those are real dangers, God is in control, and prayer is one thing we can do to have a profound effect on our children's future.

After all, God has a life plan for these kids. Although everyday stuff is important to God, He has in mind a much bigger picture than the latest head cold or stubborn streak my kid may be experiencing. In one sense, we have our children for about eighteen years, but He has them for eternity. He has a life mission for these children. He wants to develop their gifts and talents. He wants to begin, even now, to see them develop the traits of Jesus Christ Himself. He has their eternity in mind.

We parents are called to stand in the gap on behalf of our children. We are the ones who petition our almighty God to do in our children a work of eternal significance. Our faithful prayers help unlock God's character within our child, help reveal God's gifts within our child, and help steer a child's wayward heart or rebellious spirit back to God. The Bible tells us that the effectual and fervent prayers of a righteous person accomplish a great deal; this is never more true than when parents pray for their children.

Focusing Our Prayers

We parents spend a lot of time worrying about what kind of world we are leaving our children. Maybe it's time to be more concerned about what kind of inner strength and godly traits we leave to our children. While we can't change world conditions, we can help shape our children. Nancie and I began to focus our prayers on specific attributes, gifts, fruit of the Spirit, character traits, and attitudes that we knew were God's will for our children.

When we began to focus our prayers, we were surprised to see that God wanted those same characteristics in us as parents. As I prayed for our children, I realized my own weakness in many of these areas, and I began to seek these attributes for my own life.

Focusing my prayers for our children also made me more conscious of the attitudes of my family. Insight into each of my children's unique gifts began to emerge, and I was able to help clarify and encourage God's gifts within them: Jonathan's strong gift of influence and leadership; Eric's often hidden spirit of tenderness and compassion; Chris's heartfelt sense of justice and honor; Andy's wonderful warmth, smile, and gift of hospitality; and Amy's deep sense of compassion for the world's poor and downtrodden.

Grandma Ferlen

Bill and I realize that in addition to his father, several other people modeled for us what it means to be faithful in prayer. When Bill and I first met Grandma Ferlen, I thought, *What a cute little old lady*. Bill was a youth pastor in those days, and we were expecting our third child. Grandma Ferlen was eighty-nine years old. She wore a pair of thick glasses, and she always wore a hat. We soon realized, however, that this was no ordinary little old lady. Her intense blue eyes missed nothing. I found out later that she recorded prayer needs of everyone she knew. She spent hours every day sitting in her rocker, her Bible spread out on her lap, her prayer lists handy. Our family members were among hundreds on her list.

I would stop by Grandma Ferlen's house, ostensibly to cheer her up, but I really visited her because I liked being with this mighty woman of prayer. To be in her presence was to be with Jesus. I often wondered what it would take to be like her. I found her prayers would often move me to tears as I sat on a hassock next to her rocking chair with my toddlers playing nearby.

During conversation, she would lapse into prayer, and I often felt we—God, Grandma, and I—were having a three-way conversation. I remember her picking up Eric and holding him in her wrinkled arms as she prayed for him.

Grandma Ferlen died three years later, but her work of prayer made an indelible impression on my prayer life for our family. Our five children now range in age from fourteen to twenty-six years. Life is crammed full with wonderful times, painful times, scary times. I remember wondering in the scramble of taking care of small children, *Do prayers die?* I wanted desperately to believe that Grandma Ferlen's prayers were still working because I sure didn't have time for serious prayer. In the exhausted moments before I fell into bed, I often felt overwhelmed by my inadequacy. My prayers for my children felt cursory, weak, impotent.

When each of our four sons was born and when our adopted daughter, Amy, arrived from Korea, Bill and I held them close and prayed for them, reminded again of the miracle of birth and the enormous spiritual responsibility we had for each child. At one of our children's dedications, Bill sang,

> *How sweet to hold a newborn baby,*
> *And feel the pride and joy he gives.*
> *But greater still, the calm assurance,*
> *This child can face uncertain days,*
> *because He lives.*

As we stood at the altar with our children all dressed alike, we didn't know what a roller coaster of emotions, of potential for greatness and disaster would be tangled up in this package deal. However, we began to see that even if we couldn't block out large chunks of time to pray as Grandma Ferlen did, it is possible to "pray in the process" of life, to pray without ceasing for our children.

Why Do We Pray?

We pray for our children because we must pray. We are desperately needy people living in a broken world, and we have the privilege, through prayer, to connect with the Almighty, to see God intervene in our children's lives and in our own lives. God is our only hope. Through prayer, we tell Him our hearts' cry; we can hear what He has to say. Through prayer, He becomes a real friend. In opening our hearts to Him, we allow Him to lead us as we lead our children. We live in a society characterized by stunning moral decadence; we see corruption on every level of society. Apathy seems to have paralyzed hopes and dreams. Our children need a sense of vision and passion as they carry God's truth into their generation. Yesterday's rules no longer seem to apply, and we need His righteousness as never before.

We pray for our children because it is a declaration of our faith as a family. It is a profound statement to stand at the altar with our children, dedicating them to Him. In holding our children up to God, we are saying, "Father, we need You. Carry them. Carry us, as we care for them." It is a universal parental cry. Samson's father prayed after he and his wife were told they would be parents, "O my Lord, please let the Man of God whom You sent come to us again and teach us what we shall do for the child who will be born" (Judg. 13:8).

Prayer makes a significant statement, especially when it comes from those of us in leadership—whether we head a corporation, a church, or a family. Those who follow us know that we will fail them. Our children will need to forgive us as they see past our humanity to the perfect parent, to our "Abba, Father."

We parents long for safety and righteousness for our children, and that is to be found only in God's hands.

When Do We Pray?

The Bible instructs us to pray "always with all prayer and supplication in the Spirit" and to "pray without ceasing" (Eph. 6:18; 1 Thess. 5:17).

We can pray in the ordinary moments. In the most common, ordinary events of the day, we can pray for our children: in thanking God for our meals, on a summer night outside as we look at the stars together and think Big Thoughts. Before our kids go out the door to school, we can pray for them and even ask them, "What specific thing may I pray about for you today?" In the quiet moments before tucking in our children, we can kneel down, gather them in our arms or hold their hands (older kids still treasure this), and pray for them. In these receptive, intimate moments, Bill and I have often heard a child's mind and heart open up to the sacred.

As I (Nancie) write this, I realize again how fragile this sacred opportunity of prayer at bedtime is. Many bedtimes I was so exhausted that I just wanted them to go to sleep, or I was just too busy to take the time. But I remember that although bedtime prayer may seem like a tedious chore, it is a rare privilege that is holy ground. Life-changing moments are at work here.

Now that four of our children are out of the nest, we realize how short the time is for us to hold our children in our arms and pray for them. Bill and I are learning that it is essential to join hands every night and pray for our children. We pray that as we open our hands and release our children, they will choose to hold God's hand.

We can pray in the special moments. Use special events as opportunities to pray with your children. When your children graduate or go away to camp or college, take time to join hands and ask God for His protection, His touch, and His perspective on that special time. When you are on vacation, perhaps huddled together in a tent, take turns praying for each other. Thanksgiving, Christmas, Easter, and other holidays are wonderful opportunities to reflect on the true meaning of the celebration and, while the family is gathered together, to pray for each other.

We Can Make Time to Pray

Our family once had a "prayer summit." It was August 1991, and our two older sons were going away to college. One of our college-age sons was struggling with the choice of a college major, and the other had a developing relationship with a girl. Chris was going through the throes of trying to decide which colleges he should apply to, and Andy was getting ready to start high school. Amy was gathering courage for another school year, which felt like mountain climbing to her because she has severe learning disabilities. Bill was making some changes in his career, and I was again fighting with the calendar, trying to juggle priorities.

We all were feeling overwhelmed, and some jarring attitudes and tensions had surfaced in the family. What was happening to us? With all of these changes, these forks in the road, we worried: What if we get derailed and take the wrong way?

We felt as if we needed a family revival. Bill suggested that we have a one-week "family prayer summit." For one hour a day, we would gather for a special time of prayer. Finding which hour we would meet became the major challenge. With all of our schedules, it looked impossible. We nearly gave it up as a nice idea that just wouldn't work. But Bill persisted, looking at calendars, persuading, convincing, as only he can do. Finally we agreed to meet at 2:30 every afternoon for one week. So for one hour each day, we took the phone off the hook and met in the master bedroom to pray. Bill handed out copies of previously recorded prayer needs for all of us for the coming year. We both wondered if the kids would go for this. Would they balk? Would the hour drag?

Looking back upon that time, we see that it was a pivotal time in our family. In those seven hours,

we saw God move among us, gently, almost undiscernibly. We watched as the kids would get up from where they were praying and spontaneously go pray with a brother or sister or with Bill or me. As we began to pray for one another, our eyes got off our own needs and wants. Love grew as we saw each other not just as parent or child or sibling, but as another member of the body of Christ, a member whom we loved very much. During that week, we made decisions. Attitudes sweetened. Tolerance for each other's faults increased. Our vision grew as we caught a glimpse of what was really important—loving and obeying God.

How Do We Pray?

Be real, be honest in your prayer. Prayer doesn't mean we have to have a certain formula or that we must use eloquent or profound words. What is important is the honest cry from the heart. Maltie Babcock wrote, "Our prayers must mean something to us if they are to mean anything to God." The cries of the psalmist model that kind of honesty: "My soul is in anguish. How long,

O Lord, how long? Turn, O Lord, and deliver me; save me because of your unfailing love" (Ps. 6:3-4, NIV).

Sometimes it is all we can do to hold our children up to God, pleading for His mercy, His working in their lives. An honest prayer of humility out of a parent's heart is powerful. I remember when I was a little girl, I got out of bed late one night and saw my mother on her knees in front of the living-room couch. She was weeping as she prayed, and I heard her call out her children's names to God. I have never forgotten that. It was a holy moment. I remember feeling somewhat awestruck by the whole idea, not understanding it entirely. Now that I am a parent, I understand. C. S. Lewis wrote, "We must lay before him what is in us, not what ought to be in us."

Pray, and trust God with the outcome. When my father was dying of cancer, our entire family prayed. We prayed that he would be healed, and we believed that he would be. But he died. We gathered our children around us and talked about the big question marks of life. We explained that we won't always understand everything that hap-

pens, that life can be very painful, but that God never makes mistakes. He loves us, and He is with us in the pain.

We can "pray the question marks" of life. At times Bill and I wondered about the effectiveness of our prayers for our children. When Chris was twelve, a dog bit him in the mouth, and he required plastic surgery. We had prayed for safety. Why did this happen? We sent Jon on a missions trip only to see him experience disillusionment on the trip, his hopes dashed. Eric decided at one point not to go back to college (he later changed his mind). Andy needed several ear surgeries, but they were not successful. We remember praying with one of our sons over a broken heart that only God and time could heal.

If we could have stopped any of these things from happening to our children, we would have. In fact, we prayed specifically for different outcomes in each of these scenarios. But as Jean Ingelow wrote, "I have lived to thank God that all my prayers have not been answered."

Looking back, we see that God had better plans

for us than we could see at the time. He really has answered our prayers. Through these experiences we are learning compassion, patience, and trust. "Sometimes," writes Roy Pearson, "God answers our prayers in the way parents do, who reply to the pleas of their children with 'Not just now,' or 'I'll have to think about that for a while.'"

Pray with thanksgiving. As the apostle Paul sat in a Philippian jail, he wrote to his friends, "I thank my God upon every remembrance of you, always in every prayer of mine making request for you all with joy" (Phil. 1:3-4). Paul knew the secret of praying with thanksgiving. When we thank and praise God, He inhabits our praises. He is present. He draws near.

A couple of years ago I determined I would spend more intense time praying for my children. I had been concerned and worried about them, especially the older ones, who were beyond my reach. I started having nightmares about them, and it seemed that the more I prayed, the more I worried. "God, this doesn't feel very productive," I muttered and went to the Scriptures. I read, "Be anxious for nothing, but in everything by prayer and supplication, with thanksgiving, let your requests be made known to God; and the peace of God, which surpasses all understanding, will guard your hearts and minds through Christ Jesus" (Phil. 4:6-7). I realized I had been praying with foreboding, with worry instead of with thanksgiving. As I began to praise and thank God for each child, for the work He was doing in them, I experienced a new sense of peace and relinquishment in my prayers. Our children belong to God. As Hannah, Samuel's mother, said, "For this child I prayed, and the Lord has granted me my petition which I asked of Him. Therefore I also have lent him to the Lord; as long as he lives he shall be lent to the Lord" (1 Sam. 1:27-28).

Does It Matter That We Pray?

Yes. Our prayers for our children matter to God, to us, and to our children. Jesus said that people always ought to pray and not lose heart: "Shall God not avenge His own elect who cry out day and night to Him, though He bears long with them? I tell you that He will avenge them speedily. . . . When the

Son of Man comes, will He really find faith on the earth?" (Luke 18:7-8).

Persistence pays.   Often we are driven to our knees in prayer for our children because of our basic needs. We are afraid. We are in pain. We look to our "Abba, Father" to fix it, to make it better. And He does. We could fill pages with how God has intervened, protected, and led us. Jesus told the parable of the persistent widow who would not let up until the judge granted her request. Jesus used that story to illustrate how our prayers move the hand of God (Luke 18). He also said in Matthew 7:7-8: "Ask, and it will be given to you; seek, and you will find; knock, and it will be opened to you. For everyone who asks receives, and he who seeks finds, and to him who knocks it will be opened."

Prayer makes a difference! Many of us parents know that the courses of our children's lives are changed and their history is altered because of prayer. We ponder these things in our hearts, and while we are grateful for the answers, the miraculous provisions, we see that in His overall plan for us, we do not always get the answer we want in the

way we want it. These are the times we learn of God's character and what it means to wait on Him.

Prayer warriors are made, not born. When I get to heaven, I'm going to ask Grandma Ferlen how it was when her children were young. When did she start seeing that prayer was a worthy work? When Grandma Ferlen died, she left me her tattered old Bible that was filled with notes. I think of all the years she spent praying over her Bible, writing down prayer needs as well as the answers in the margins. I think that as she walked with God through the years, as she moved through the process of life, she grew to love Him so much that she spent more and more time with Him.

That's what I want to do too. Prayer changes us. In prayer, we enter God's presence, and He changes us.

Fasting and Prayer

The Bible encourages us to consider that some situations may require prayer and fasting. "This kind does not go out except by prayer and fasting" (Matt. 17:21). When fasting is mentioned in the Bible, it is often because the problem or circumstance seems overwhelming; the desperation to see God intervene has reached a fever pitch. We parents sometimes feel that way. At times the problems or circumstances surrounding our children seem to be overwhelming. We are at our wits' end and have exhausted our own resourcefulness in dealing with the situation.

If that is the case, God may be calling us to fast and pray. Some things require us to break the pattern of our prayer life and dig a little deeper. At times we reach a stalemate. We recognize that the children for whom we pray and whom we love are in a struggle beyond their ability to cope. It could be a strong-willed, rebellious issue. It could be the influence of peer pressure taking them down the wrong path. It could be a physical or emotional illness. It could be a deep hurt that all of our comfort won't heal. No matter the problem, something within us tells us that "this kind does not go out except by prayer and fasting."

Sometimes these things require frequent or prolonged fasting. Bill and I have fasted for every one of our children at one time or another, and we have seen positive results.

You will know when it is time to pray and fast for your child. God's Spirit will tell you. We encourage you to respond to God's voice urging you to fast. No one else can or will stand in the gap for your child. That is your privilege and responsibility as a caring, praying parent.

Why We Wrote This Book

Like you, we continue to face hectic schedules and what seems to be an all-consuming agenda. This very week that we are sending off the first draft of this book to the publisher, we seem to have so many demands and so little time. It has been this way since our children were small: laundry to do, meals to fix, jobs to go to, school activities, church activities, piano lessons, basketball games, letters to write, bills to pay, phone calls to make, yards to weed, garages to clean—well, you know.

This book is not an interruption or a nagging side note to what is going on at our house now. Rather it is at the heart of where we are now. In the midst of confusion, growth, and change—as we watch our children leave home to attend college, start careers, and get married—we are reminded of the importance of a parent's prayer.

The character traits and attitudes that form the focus of our prayers for our children are qualities that build good character into their lives, helping them become people of morality, integrity, and wisdom. These qualities do not come easily or naturally to any of us.

While we desire to see these qualities grow in our children, we are not always open to the ways God may choose to develop those qualities. As adults we know that it is often the difficulties that drive us headlong into God's presence and into His Word. We learn when we are up against the wall, when we are desperate and needy, when we are lonely or in the wilderness.

We do not naturally want difficulties for our children. It is our tendency to shield them from danger, to protect them from harm, to provide for their needs, and to "rescue" them. Their cries are painful for us to hear. We want to fix things for them, to kiss away the hurts, and to soothe their fears.

At certain points in our children's lives, that's exactly what we are called to do. But as parents with a godly vision, we want higher, better things for our children. We want them to know and love God.

So we offer the prayers in this book with this spirit:

Lord, we want our children to know You because to know You is life eternal. Bring our children to You, dear God. Do Your work so thoroughly in us that our lives as parents are to them a prayer. This is the only truly worthwhile legacy we can give them—that You are indeed God to us and that as they dig out their own wells on their journeys, You will be God to them. You will be to them like living water in a dry and thirsty land.

Bill and Nancie Carmichael

To help you use this book most effectively, let us explain some of our goals and thoughts. You will find fifty-two chapters in this book—one for every week in the year, if you choose to use it that way. Each chapter focuses on one specific character trait, attribute, or quality that will form the basis of your prayers for your child or children.

The list of fifty-two attributes is not an exhaustive list, and it is not necessarily the list of the best fifty-two attributes. After you become familiar with the concept and flow of this book, you can add other attributes and qualities to pray for with your child. In many ways this book is a sample, a model that you can expand.

We want this book to be a useful tool. We hope you spend time in it every day. You may want to pray the opening prayer and study the Scripture passages on one day; read the reflections another day; study the quotations a third day. Use the book in whatever way fits in with the rhythm of your life.

Ideally the book will help you focus your prayers, move you to a deeper level of praying for your children, open your eyes to ways God is working in your children, and help your children grow in godliness. We encourage you to *use* this book in the fullest sense. Allow it to give voice to your heart cries for your children. Write in it. Add things to it. Record your thoughts and prayers. Allow it to become a written witness to God's faithfulness in your family.

To help you understand the function of the separate sections of each chapter, we'll walk you through a typical chapter.

Prayer

The opening prayer helps you start thinking about the specific attribute covered in that chapter. This prayer can be used as a springboard for you to begin your own prayers about the attribute. We believe that prayer is conversation with God. In that conversation we can say anything we feel about the attribute. We can confess our fears and frustrations. We can acknowledge our own weaknesses. We can let God know we don't know how to approach the subject. And we can include specific things we know about our child and his or her aptitude for this particular attribute.

You may begin by using this prayer as your prayer if it feels comfortable, or you can use it as a thought process to spark your own prayer.

Scripture

We included Scripture passages that give some insight about the specific attribute. Again, use these verses as sparks to ignite your own interest in what Scripture teaches about the attribute. You may want to do your own word-search study to find significant passages. These verses are for your meditation. In Psalm 1, David tells us that it is delightful to meditate on the Word of the Lord. To meditate means to contemplate, to ponder, to reflect, or to chew on. As you "chew on" these Scripture passages, the Lord will bring new insight to you. As you do a chore, drive to work, or wait for the copy machine to warm up, engage your mind in a meditative moment on the Scripture verses chosen for each attribute.

Insight

We have attempted to make the attribute more real by sharing personal illustrations and reflections. We hope that these reflections will inspire you with insight, conviction, and added knowledge. You may find the reflections useful if you discuss the attribute with your child.

We have also added a simple prayer that is a more specific synopsis of what we are praying for. It is given to help you focus on the specific attribute of the week.

Reflection

Because we have always learned from what other people say about a subject, we have included quotations from other sources. Some quotations are from classic works of men and women who pondered these thoughts many years ago, and some are from our contemporaries who live a hectic pace in our culture.

Family Interaction

We offer here some conversation starters and other ideas that may help you discuss with your children the attribute you are praying about each week. This interaction can happen at the dinner table, during family devotion times, or just in private conversation with your child. They are meant to stimulate ideas on how to introduce your children to this attribute and let them know what you are praying for this week.

Because each child is unique, you will need to adapt the interaction to fit each child's needs and level of understanding. Most children are curious and have a natural desire to learn. The idea is to spend time conveying the concept to your children so that they can understand what God is trying to do in their lives.

Communicating the Blessing

This is not a prayer (although you can make it one if you choose to do so). Rather it is a blessing you can convey to your children sometime during the week. Again, choose a time that is natural for you and your children: before bedtime prayers, during family devotions, or as you ride in the car together. With this statement you let your children know that you are praying for them, asking God to develop His character within them, and you explain to them the meaning of the particular attribute.

You might also want to include a compliment. For example, if the attribute for the week is compassion and you observe your child in an act of compassion (it could be with family pets, dolls, or a sibling), affirm the compassion you see the child expressing and remind the child that showing compassion is reflecting God's character. Indicate that you are praying for God to develop His compassion in him or her.

My Prayer for My Child

This journal space is for you to write your own prayers, contemplations, Scripture verses, and thoughts about the attribute. Write down what you see developing in your children. You may want to include a short entry for each child. Record your child's particular needs and your specific prayer request for each child. Record the day's date with your request.

Follow-up Prayers, Answers, and Insights

Use this space to write your reflections on your children's growth a month or a year after you have first prayed for them. Note the progress made or new insights you may have. Note how God answered your prayers and what circumstances or people He used. Again, record the day's date.

If you see significant growth in a particular area in your child or children, make sure to do two things: Thank God for His work in your children's lives, and tell your child or children what growth you see.

This space and the one above will help you estab-

lish a prayer journal that will provide insight into both your children's character development and God's character. The journal will be a record of God's faithfulness to reveal Himself in and through your children. You will find it rewarding to read the journal several years from now.

Keepsake Prayer Journal—Pass On the Legacy

When you complete this book, you may want to pass it on to your child as a record of God's faithfulness. You may want to fill out a book for each of your children.

As we mentioned before, in this keepsake prayer journal, you do two things: You lay your requests on the altar, submitting them to God's mercy; and you erect a memorial to God's faithfulness in your child's life, so that when your child asks at a later time, "What do these prayers mean?" you can share the story of how God revealed His character in and through your child's life.

May the Lord who blesses children bless you as you enter this commitment to pray for your child and as you erect this memorial to His glory.

LORD, HELP MY CHILD TO LEARN . . .

Compassion

Contentment

Gentleness

Gratitude

Honesty

Humility

Obedience

Persistence

Responsibility

PART *1*

LORD, HELP MY CHILD TO LEARN ...

COMPASSION

1

But when [Jesus] saw the multitudes, He was moved with compassion for them,

because they were weary and scattered, like sheep having no shepherd.

Matthew 9:36

P R A Y E R

Lord, Your very nature is compassion. You see all of life through eyes of love and grace and mercy. Help my child see the world through Your eyes, to be touched not just in the pocketbook but in his or her heart. Help my child love the unlovely, the dirty, the homeless, the addicted, the aged. Help my child to extend forgiveness and mercy to those who don't seem to deserve it. Help my child's hands to reach out with healing in Your name. Help me too, Lord, to be an example to my child by serving others with Your heart of compassion.

"But You, O Lord, are a God full of compassion, and gracious, longsuffering and abundant in mercy and truth" (Ps. 86:15).

When I (Nancie) was a child, my mother used to catch us up with a hug and a smile once in a while and ask, "What's it like to be you?" Compassion comes from simply wondering and caring: What is it like to be you? What pressures are you feeling? Why are you feeling pressure? Where do you hurt? How can I be your friend?

Frederick Buechner wrote, "Compassion is the sometimes fatal capacity for feeling what it is like to live inside somebody else's skin. It is the knowledge that there can never really be any peace and joy for me until there is peace and joy for you too."

What is compassion? It is Jesus coming to earth to be like us, to identify with our human experience. One of His greatest desires is that we show the same compassion to others, that we show mercy and ease suffering.

As we look at Jesus' life on earth, we see how He moved among people, touching their hurts, healing them. His very life's message is compassion. He taught us in Matthew 25:35-

36, 40: "I was hungry and you gave Me food; I was thirsty and you gave Me drink; I was a stranger and you took Me in; I was naked and you clothed Me; I was sick and you visited Me; I was in prison and you came to Me. . . . Assuredly, I say to you, inasmuch as you did it to one of the least of these My brethren, you did it to Me."

Jesus still moves among us and shows His compassion to us, regardless of our status, our race, or our gender. As our High Priest, He sympathizes with our weaknesses and understands our temptations (Heb. 4:15).

Compassion does not come naturally to us. We are by nature self-centered. It takes time and a work of God's grace to develop compassion. Some children, depending on their temperaments, learn compassion easier than others do.

We learn compassion either by going through certain circumstances or by trying to imagine what other people are going through. Our daughter, Amy, was an abandoned child and spent the first three years of her life in an orphan-

Compassion

age in Korea. Whenever she sees pictures of starving or homeless children, she is moved. When we are in the city, she cannot bear to pass any beggar on the street without putting some money into an outstretched hand or cup. She feels compassion because she knows instinctively what it is like to be homeless, to be hungry. The old saying "Never judge another until you've walked a mile in his moccasins" really is true. When we go through the death of a friend or family member, an illness, or a trying time, we often discover that the people who come alongside us and help the most are the people who either have experienced the same difficulties or try to understand what we are going through without feeling a need to fix it or make judgments.

Compassion reaches into hearts and lives, past barriers, past judgment, and brings the touch of God.

I pray that my children will be ever more like Jesus. I pray that when they see needs in the world around them they will be moved with compassion. I also pray that they will know God's compassion in their own lives. Help me as a parent to be His heart and voice and arms of compassion to my children.

REFLECTION

"Living the sacrament of care for others draws a person close to the greatest of all truths. It does this better than anything else can, but it does this in ways that are seldom obvious. It is for this reason that it is a spiritual discipline."

Ernest Boyer, Jr., *A Way in the World*

"Our limited acts of love reveal to us His unlimited love. Our small gestures of care reveal His boundless care. Our fearful and hesitant words reveal His fearless and guiding Word. It is indeed through our broken, vulnerable, mortal ways of being that the healing power of the eternal God becomes visible to us. Therefore, we are called each day to present to our Lord the whole of our lives."

Henri Nouwen, *A Cry for Mercy*

"What doth hinder us? . . . What but the presence of a veil in our hearts? . . . It is woven of the fine threads of the self-life, the hyphenated sins of the human spirit. They are not something we do, they are something we are. . . . Self-righteousness, self-pity, self-confidence, self-sufficiency, self-admiration, and a host of others like them."

A. W. Tozer, *The Pursuit of God*

FAMILY INTERACTION

1 Ask your child, "What does it feel like to be you?" Really listen.

2 Discuss with your child how each of you can become more compassionate.

3 Talk with your child about an ethnic group or a certain class of people. How might preconceived ideas and prejudices affect how we view them?

4 Say to your child, "Name someone you dislike or have a hard time getting along with. Now, try to put yourself in that person's place." If your child has a hard time doing that, do the exercise yourself, showing your child how to think empathetically and compassionately. Pray together with your child for this person.

COMMUNICATING THE BLESSING

I pray for you, my child, to show compassion by blessing those who need God's blessing most and by remembering that other people often suffer deep pain or problems we do not understand. I pray that you will not allow preconceived ideas or snap judgments to rule your attitude toward others, but instead, that you will allow God's compassion to flow through you.

MY PRAYER FOR MY CHILD

NAME _____ DATE _____

_____

_____

FOLLOW-UP PRAYERS, ANSWERS, AND INSIGHTS

NAME _____ DATE _____

_____

_____

LORD, HELP MY CHILD TO LEARN . . .

CONTENTMENT

Godliness with contentment is great gain.

1 Timothy 6:6

2

PRAYER

Lord, in this age of materialism, insatiable appetites, and pleasure run wild, we are so programmed not to be content. Help my child see the futility of pursuing things and sensations. Help my child understand that contentment comes not from great wealth but from fewer wants. Give my child an appetite for learning truth. And help me to demonstrate contentment in my own lifestyle.

SCRIPTURE

"I have learned to be content whatever the circumstances" (Phil. 4:11, NIV).

Some years ago, when our sons were young, we went out for ice cream after a Little League game to celebrate a win. The three older boys all got double scoops of ice cream. Andy, then only two years old, tended to put most of his ice cream on the outside of his face, so we ordered him a single scoop. Andy noticed the raw deal he was getting and sent up a howl. It wasn't fair. They all got two scoops, and he got only one! Chris, the family sage, advised his baby brother, "Andy, be thankful for what you get!"

Being thankful for what we have, knowing it is from our Father's hand, is the key to contentment. Our contentment gets rattled when we compare what we have with what others have. Children are pressured to compare labels of clothes and shoes, bikes, Rollerblades, computer games, cars, colleges, homes, vacations. The list grows as we go through life, and we can never seem to find a stopping place. We all know what is best, and we want it.

But in this mad pursuit of things, we can lose sight of what is essential. Verses from the New Testament ask us to examine ourselves: "Do you look at things according to the outward appearance? . . . For we dare not class ourselves or compare ourselves with those who commend themselves. But they, measuring themselves by themselves, and comparing

Contentment

themselves among themselves, are not wise" (2 Cor. 10:7, 12).

It is not wise to compare ourselves to other people. We will always find someone who appears to be better, to have more. Then a sense of competition can take over, and we are off to "win."

What a challenge it is to help our children be content. We Americans in our market-driven culture tend not to be a contented bunch. We can easily become consumed with succeeding, with wanting more—even among Christians, even within the church. And there is a fine line between ambition and greed. "Find the need and fill it" defines much of what we do. Lethargy, apathy, or laziness are not the things we want for our children. We want our children to see that we live with a view toward eternity. Colossians 3:2 encourages us to set our affection on "things above, not on things on the earth."

So what does it mean to be content? What does it mean for us who are the upwardly mobile of the world, who are always looking for a better way, a way to grow, a way to succeed? In *The Book of Virtues,* William J. Bennett writes, "The ancient Greeks had a saying, 'Nothing overmuch.' The maxim calls not for total abstinence, but rather reminds us to avoid excess. We should know that too much of anything, even a good thing, may prove to be our undoing. . . . We need to recognize when enough is enough."

Posted on our refrigerator is this saying: "Things don't last. People do." This helps us discern where the lines get crossed in our pursuit of things. When our relationships with God and other people are suffering from our pursuit of things and success, then we must back off and check our priorities.

When we as parents are tempted to compare our children with other people's children— Are our children as athletic, as smart, as well behaved, as spiritual as others'?—we must draw the line. These subtle comparisons are destructive. *What we have is from the Father's hand.* It is what we do with what we have been given that counts.

I pray that my children will learn godliness with contentment, and that in doing so, they will become satisfied with what God gives them.

R E F L E C T I O N

"When thou hast Christ, thou art rich and hast enough. He will be thy faithful and provident helper in all things, so that thou shall not need to trust in men. For men quickly change and quickly fail; but Christ remaineth forever and standeth by us firmly to the end."

Thomas à Kempis, *The Imitation of Christ*

"Lord, let my life be orderly, regular, temperate; let no pride or self-seeking, no covetousness or revenge, no little ends and low imaginations pollute my spirit and unhallow my words and actions. Let my body be a servant of my spirit and both my body and spirit be servants of Jesus, doing all things for your glory here. Amen."

Jeremy Taylor

"I look back on my life like a good day's work; it was done, and I feel satisfied with it. I was happy and contented . . . and life is what we make it, always has been, always will be."

Grandma Moses, artist and mother of ten children

FAMILY INTERACTION

1 Ask your child, "If you could buy anything you wanted right now, what would it be?" Discuss with your child that while the stuff we buy may give us pleasure for a little while, it is the things we can't buy that give us lasting satisfaction. Discuss the valuable things we can't buy: love, friendship, salvation, encouragement, laughter, wisdom, joy, confidence, etc.

2 Read Philippians 4:8, and ask your child to list several noble, just, pure, lovely, good, virtuous, and praiseworthy things about your family. Turn this list into a prayer of thanks for all God has given you.

3 Ask your child to come to dinner with a list of the three possessions that mean the most to him or her.

COMMUNICATING THE BLESSING

I pray for you, my child, to learn contentment with the things that God gives to you and to have control of things rather than allowing things to control you.

MY PRAYER FOR MY CHILD

NAME _____ DATE _____

_____

_____

FOLLOW-UP PRAYERS, ANSWERS, AND INSIGHTS

NAME _____ DATE _____

_____

_____

LORD, HELP MY CHILD TO LEARN . . .

GENTLENESS

3

A servant of the Lord must not quarrel but be gentle to all, able to teach, patient.

2 Timothy 2:24

PRAYER

Lord, let my child learn the great strength there is in gentleness, a fruit of Your Spirit. Let my child be one who wants to heal broken things. Give my child the ability to whisper Your words of comfort and encouragement to the wounded and downtrodden. Help my child see the joy in spending time with children, with those who are lonely. Teach my child to listen with compassion.

SCRIPTURE

"But the wisdom that is from above is first pure, then peaceable, gentle, willing to yield, full of mercy and good fruits, without partiality and without hypocrisy" (James 3:17).

1

Have you seen gentleness lately? It's a rare quality these days.

Four years ago, a scrawny black-and-white stray cat showed up at our house. He was starving and terrified of people. He hid under the far reaches of our deck, darting out only now and then for scraps of food that Amy fed him. Amy thought for sure her prayers for a cat had been answered, and every day after school, she would sit patiently on the edge of the deck, offering food and gentle reassurances. Gradually Spooky began to trust Amy as he realized she would not hurt him. It was beautiful to see how her gentle manner convinced Spooky that he was home. Spooky pretty much has the run of the place now, trusting and cuddling all of us.

We tend to think of gentleness as weakness. We see it as passive and insipid in nature. Nothing could be further from the truth. Galatians 5:22-23 says, "But the fruit of the Spirit is . . . gentleness." A gentle spirit is evidence of a submissive walk with God, a personality molded and controlled by God. Consider Jesus, the essence of gentleness. In righteous anger He overturned the money-changers' tables in the temple. He healed the sick, fed the hungry, and taught eternal truths. The ultimate example of His gentle-

ness was in facing the Cross, laying down His life when He could have called in legions of angels and spared Himself the agony of the Crucifixion.

We pray for gentleness for our children because it means having a heart turned toward God and others. Gentleness is an openness to others, a willingness to learn, to reach toward someone else without defenses. Gentleness is difficult to describe but reveals itself in a temperament under submission to God. In a culture obsessed with individual significance, with being successful, with being right, we tend to see aggression and power as virtues. Some sports heroes and movie characters exemplify these characteristics in their macho, rude, and violent behavior.

But gentleness is strong love: power under submission. Gentleness toward another person is true respect for the other. In gentleness I acknowledge that God has uniquely created *you* and that I am to tread softly when I encounter you because you are made in His image. Gentleness means that I can choose to love you. Gentleness is choosing love over impatience, expedience, or judgment. "Love . . . does not behave rudely, does not seek its own, is not provoked" (1 Cor. 13:4-5).

In teaching our children this beautiful quality, we see that it is something that is caught, not taught. The expression in our eyes toward our children is very powerful, and just by the way we look at them or talk to them, we can communicate a gentle or hard spirit. Proverbs 27:19 says, "As in water face reflects face, so a man's heart reveals the man."

Gentleness is a challenge for us parents. In our desire to be good parents, we can come across to our children as hard. An approachable parent—strong and respected—has gentleness at his or her core. People feel safe with gentle people. The apostle Paul speaks of this nurturing, loving quality as he uses this metaphor: "But we were gentle among you, like a mother caring for her little children" (1 Thess. 2:7, NIV).

I pray that my children will learn the enormous strength inherent in a gentle spirit, a spirit in submission to the Holy Spirit.

R E F L E C T I O N

"Gentleness is Thy work, my God, and it is the work Thou hast given me to do."

François Fénelon

"Take time to be tender. Fragile and delicate are the feelings of most who seek our help. They need to sense we are there because we care, not just because it's our job."

Charles Swindoll, *Growing Strong in the Seasons of Life*

"In learning to be controlled [by God] we don't approach Him wondering what He owes us; we seek to discover what we owe Him. Neither do we demand privileges to make our life easier; we embrace demanding responsibilities instead, giving all rights to God."

Judith Lechman, *The Spirituality of Gentleness*

F A M I L Y I N T E R A C T I O N

1 Babies, puppies, and kittens make great conversation starters for discussions about gentleness. Let your child hold a small animal or see a tiny baby. Visit a pet shop if you do not have baby animals. It's natural for your child to want to be gentle with any of the above.

Gentleness

2 After the experience, discuss what it feels like to be gentle. Remind your child that he or she could have been rough or even hurtful with the tiny animal or baby. Explain to your child that being gentle is choosing to be careful and considerate, keeping ourselves under control. Remind your child that gentleness is a fruit of God's Spirit.

3 If the opportunity arises (and if you have more than one child around, it will!) during conflict or sibling rivalry, discuss what it means to respect one another's boundaries. Talk about how being gentle with one another shows love and respect for yourself and for others.

COMMUNICATING THE BLESSING

I pray for you, my child, to cultivate gentleness. Remember that the open hands of friendship accomplish far more in this life than the clenched fists of anger.

MY PRAYER FOR MY CHILD

NAME _____ DATE _____

_____

_____

_____

_____

FOLLOW-UP PRAYERS, ANSWERS, AND INSIGHTS

NAME _____ DATE _____

_____

_____

_____

LORD, HELP MY CHILD TO LEARN...

GRATITUDE

4

Rejoice always, pray without ceasing, in everything give thanks;

for this is the will of God in Christ Jesus for you.

1 Thessalonians 5:16-18

PRAYER

Lord, I pray that my child will develop a grateful heart. Thank You for reminding us that having a spirit of gratitude and thanksgiving toward You is a doorway into Your presence. Help me to demonstrate gratitude in my own life. Help us in this self-absorbed generation to give You joyful thanks.

SCRIPTURE

"And let the peace of God rule in your hearts, to which also you were called in one body; and be thankful. . . . And whatever you do in word or deed, do all in the name of the Lord Jesus, giving thanks to God the Father through Him" (Col. 3:15, 17).

We were sitting in the airport boarding area, waiting for our flight to be called. Timmy, whom we guessed to be about three years old, was the focus of attention in the area. He was what you might call a pistol—climbing everywhere, running, asking a dozen questions, wanting drinks and trips to the bathroom, and in general exhausting his patient parents, who were also caring for a small baby. We were amused, remembering the toddler days in our family.

The flight attendant at the desk pulled a little toy airplane out of somewhere and offered it to Timmy as a diversion. Timmy's mother hovered over him, instructing, "Say thank you, Timmy."

Timmy hesitated, rolling his big brown eyes up at the attendant. The whole waiting area waited, breathless, in this moment of high drama: Would Timmy say thank you?

After more prodding from his mother and father, Timmy finally lisped, "Thank you," and everyone in the waiting room breathed a collective sigh of relief as Timmy sat down to play with his airplane.

We want so much to teach our children to say please and thank you. Saying thank you

helps to generate a gracious attitude toward others. Saying thank you reminds us that all we have has been given to us. A spirit of gratitude toward God is a simple but powerful statement: "God, You *are,* and You have given me good things. I am grateful. I praise You." The writer of Hebrews put it this way: "Let us continually offer the sacrifice of praise to God, that is, the fruit of our lips, giving thanks to His name" (Heb. 13:15).

Gratitude, the strongest weapon against pride, eludes us when we compare ourselves to other people: "Hey. No fair! If only I had the talent or the money or the home he or she has." Gratitude is really a statement of faith: *God, I trust You with my life. I trust You to give me what You think I can handle. I will trust You with the outcome, and in the midst of life, I will praise You.* The psalmist wrote, "I will bless the Lord at all times; His praise shall continually be in my mouth" (Ps. 34:1).

We are learning as a family, through the good times and the bad, that *God is in everything.* Sometimes the very best gifts He gives us are ones we do not want or have not asked for. But something wonderful happens when we look to Him and say thank you, when we realize that He has given us the very air we breathe, last night's rest, the new day. Albert

Schweitzer wrote, "We must look outward with wonder and upward with gratitude."

A life of gratitude is the doorway into God's presence. The psalmist wrote, "Enter into His gates with thanksgiving, and into His courts with praise. Be thankful to Him, and bless His name" (Ps. 100:4).

In all of life God shows His mercy toward us, His steadfast love.

I pray that my children will develop grateful hearts, that somehow in the midst of life they will begin to comprehend God's astonishing goodness. And in being grateful to Him, I pray that they will have a new awareness of His presence.

REFLECTION

"I must be continually astonished at God's goodness to me."

Brother Lawrence, *The Practice of the Presence of God*

"To be grateful is to recognize the love of God in everything He has given us— and He has given us everything. Every breath we draw is a gift of His love, every moment of existence is a gift of grace, for it brings with it immense graces from Him. Gratitude therefore takes nothing for granted, is never unresponsive, is constantly awakening to new wonder and to praise of the goodness of God."

Thomas Merton, *Thoughts in Solitude*

"The gifts of grace cannot flow in us, because we are unthankful to the giver and return them not wholly to the source and the fountain. For grace ever attendeth him that is duly thankful."

Thomas à Kempis, *Imitation of Christ*

FAMILY INTERACTION

1 Share with your child some things or people for whom you are grateful. Explain why you are grateful. Then ask your child to do the same. Turn your list into a prayer of thanks.

2 Discuss with your child some of the things that you have been given, things you have not earned. To whom will you give thanks for these things?

3 What is the difference between complaining and sharing honest emotions?

4 Share with one another answers to prayer and God's miraculous provision in the past.

5 Describe a recent setback or adversity, and discuss how you can give thanks even while you are in the midst of the difficulty.

COMMUNICATING THE BLESSING

I pray for you, my child, to learn gratitude. I pray that you will cultivate a grateful heart that does not forget God's benefits but instead recognizes that He is the Creator and giver of all things. I pray that you will also remember to offer gratitude toward others, knowing that every good gift comes from God.

MY PRAYER FOR MY CHILD

NAME _____ DATE _____

_____

_____

_____

_____

FOLLOW-UP PRAYERS, ANSWERS, AND INSIGHTS

NAME _____ DATE _____

_____

_____

_____

_____

LORD, HELP MY CHILD TO LEARN...

HONESTY

5

Behold, You desire truth in the inward parts, and in the hidden part

You will make me to know wisdom.

Psalm 51:6

PRAYER

Lord, it's so easy to cheat. I pray that my child will not only practice honesty but also love honesty. I pray that my child will not only speak truthfully but also live truthfully. Help my child to have the humility to be truthful about himself or herself and to be honest in dealing with other people, knowing that You are the great discerner of hearts and intentions.

SCRIPTURE

"I have no greater joy than to hear that my children walk in truth" (3 John 1:4).

Honesty

Kids can spot dishonesty a mile away. A few years ago, I (Nancie) was experiencing some health problems. I did my best to keep up with the family, but I did my share of complaining and moaning in private. One day after company had left, Andy (age fourteen at the time) said, "Mom, how come when company is here, you act all cheery, then when they leave, you act all sick?" I didn't have a good answer for him. He had spotted my behavior as phony, and he had a point. I was giving outsiders my best, saving my worst for the family.

It is amazing how clever we become at protecting and enhancing ourselves, how creative we become at justifying dishonesty. I (Bill) love ice cream. When I was a little boy, we lived around the corner from an ice-cream store. One day when my little brother Jimmy and I went to Woody's for ice cream, we only had enough money for one cone. After we left the store with our one ice-cream cone, I came up with a plan: I sent Jimmy back to tell Woody we had dropped the ice-cream cone. It worked. True to his kind-hearted nature, Woody dished up another ice-cream cone. I was delighted . . . until I told my mother of my clever plan. She marched me back into Woody's and made me confess my dishonesty and make it right.

It seems that cheating has become the rule rather than the exception: shoplifting, adultery, as well as cheating on income tax, insurance claims, and final exams are a few items in the everybody-does-it category. Now taxpayers must pay billions because once-respected savings and loan officers decided to get rich at someone else's expense.

To live honestly is to go against the grain of our culture. But we must remind our families: Not *everyone* is cheating. God has called us to be salt and light in this world. With His help we must walk honestly and uprightly.

The best way to practice honesty is to admit when we're dishonest. I (Nancie) had to admit to Andy that he was right: I was being dishonest in my expressions of how I felt. When we admit our failures and ask forgiveness, it helps us to remember the next time we're tempted to shade the truth.

I pray that my children will be honest. First, I pray that they will be honest to God, owning up to where they are with Him. Second, I pray that they will be honest with themselves, knowing that recognizing the truth about ourselves sets us free. Finally, I pray that they will be honest in their dealings with other people, reflecting God's truth and honesty in their lives.

R E F L E C T I O N

"Deep down in me I knowed it was a lie, and He knowed it.
You can't pray a lie—I found that out."

Huck Finn in Mark Twain's *The Adventures of Huckleberry Finn*

"Even a broken clock tells the truth twice a day!"

Anonymous

"How desperately difficult it is to be honest with oneself.
It is much easier to be honest with other people."

Edward Benson

"We strive continually to adorn and preserve our imaginary self,
neglecting the true one!"

Pascal

F A M I L Y   I N T E R A C T I O N

Honesty

1 Read with your child a story about honesty. You will find several stories in William J. Bennett's *The Book of Virtues*. Then discuss with your child an area in which you struggle with honesty. Encourage your child to discuss a struggle with honesty in his or her life.

2 Discuss a situation in which someone was dishonest with you. Tell your child how that dishonesty made you feel. Ask your child to share a similar story.

3 Discuss how we are hindered from becoming all we can in Christ by these lies:
- I am inferior (or superior) to you.
- I don't have any problems.
- If I tell you the real truth, you won't like the real me.

COMMUNICATING THE BLESSING

I pray for you, my child, to learn honesty. I pray that you will tell the truth, pay and earn an honest day's wages, give the government what you owe, avoid get-rich-quick schemes, be faithful to your spouse, and play fair. Be open to God and transparent with other people. If you are always truthful, you will never have to worry about remembering what you said to anyone. If you are always honest, you will be able to look in the mirror and see the real you.

MY PRAYER FOR MY CHILD

NAME _____ DATE _____

_____

_____

_____

_____

_____

_____

Honesty

FOLLOW-UP PRAYERS, ANSWERS, AND INSIGHTS

NAME _____ DATE _____

_____

_____

_____

_____

_____

LORD, HELP MY CHILD TO LEARN . . .

*H*UMILITY

6

God resists the proud, but gives grace to the humble. . . . Humble yourselves in the

sight of the Lord, and He will lift you up.

James 4:6, 10

P R A Y E R

Lord, Your Word declares that we are to come to You empty, ready to be filled with Your power and righteousness. I ask that my child have the willingness to be emptied of pride, self-righteousness, and self-pity. Holy Father, break, melt, and shape my child into a vessel of honor.

S C R I P T U R E

"Jesus, knowing that the Father had given all things into His hands, and that He had come from God and was going to God, . . . began to wash the disciples' feet" (John 13:3-5).

Our oldest son, Jon, has always been a dedicated competitor. His goal to get to the state basketball finals was realized twice while he was in high school. During those heady days, Jon frequently quoted this verse: "Before honor is humility" (Prov. 15:33). Jon knew that pride comes before a fall and that humility must come before any honors because honors are transitory and fleeting.

It is a natural tendency to want to believe that our gifts and accomplishments are our own doing. We live in a culture obsessed with individual significance, and this drives us in many ways. It feels good to have others tell us we are talented, beautiful, or smart. It is easy to begin to believe our own "press releases" instead of practicing humility and recognizing that God is the giver of all gifts.

Humility is not "worm" theology, a sense of worthlessness. Mother Teresa in *The Love of Christ* defines humility this way: "Humility is nothing but the truth. 'What have we got that we have not received?' asks St. Paul. If I have received everything what good have I on my own? If we are convinced of this, we will never raise our heads in pride."

Humility is a result of knowing ourselves— our weaknesses as well as our strengths—and knowing God. Sometimes we think of humility as an evasive quality that leaves the moment we identify it. That is not true. As Thomas Merton wrote in *Thoughts in Solitude*:

> Humility is a virtue, not a neurosis. It sets us free to act virtuously, to serve God, and to know Him. Therefore true humility can never inhibit any really virtuous action, nor can it prevent us from fulfilling ourselves by doing the will of God.

> Humility sets us free to do what is really good, by showing us our illusions and withdrawing our will from what was only an apparent good.

> A humility that freezes our being and frustrates all healthy activity is not humility at all, but a disguised form of pride. It dries up the roots of the spiritual life and makes it impossible for us to give ourselves to God.

I pray that my children will learn humility and in the learning of it will be aware of the Lord's strength, which is made perfect in their weakness.

REFLECTION

"I long to accomplish a great and noble task, but it is my chief duty to accomplish humble tasks as though they were great and noble. The world is moved along not only by the mighty shoves of its heroes, but also by the aggregate of the tiny pushes of each honest worker."

Helen Keller

"Filter everything through the same question: Will this bring glory to God or to me?"

Charles Swindoll, *Rise and Shine*

"Prayer is essentially man standing before his God in wonder, awe, and humility; man, made in the image of God, responding to his maker."

George Appleton

"The most earnest workers for God are those who have made enough mistakes to make them humble."

Anonymous

Humility

FAMILY INTERACTION

1 Discuss with your child a situation in which a person bragged a lot (some people, like Muhammad Ali, do it as an act). Why is it wrong to boast or brag?

2 When are you tempted to boast or brag? Discuss that this often happens when we are feeling inferior.

3 Discuss with your child a situation in which a person acted with humility. What was appealing about the person's behavior?

4 Discuss with your child ways in which you both can practice humility.

COMMUNICATING THE BLESSING

I pray for you, my child, to learn humility, knowing who you are and knowing who God is. May you see that your source of worth is in Christ. May you recognize that it is only in acknowledging your emptiness and weakness that Christ is able to be strong in you.

MY PRAYER FOR MY CHILD

NAME _____ DATE _____

_____

_____

_____

_____

_____

Humility

FOLLOW-UP ANSWERS, PRAYERS, AND INSIGHTS

NAME _____ DATE _____

_____

_____

_____

_____

_____

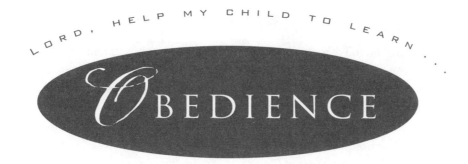

LORD, HELP MY CHILD TO LEARN...

OBEDIENCE

7

Has the Lord as great delight in burnt offerings and sacrifices, as in obeying the

voice of the Lord? Behold, to obey is better than sacrifice.

1 Samuel 15:22

PRAYER

Lord, I pray that my child will learn obedience to those You've placed as guides in his or her life. Lord, I realize that I have often wanted my child to be obedient about something for self-serving reasons—so that my life would be easier as a parent. But God, I pray for a higher law of obedience—for my child's heart to be turned toward You, because You know what is best. I pray for courage and insight to teach my child these important lessons, as my own heart turns toward You.

"For You do not desire sacrifice, or else I would give it; You do not delight in burnt offering. The sacrifices of God are a broken spirit, a broken and a contrite heart—these, O God, You will not despise" (Ps. 51:16-17).

I N S I G H T

When we are young and full of ideas and passions run high, it can be hard to see obedience as the best thing for us. Obedience can feel restrictive, punitive. But obedience to God and to those He has placed in authority over us offers protection, a set of safe boundaries in which to grow and develop. Obedience is part of God's plan for our fulfillment. Ephesians 6:1-4 says, "Children, obey your parents in the Lord, for this is right. 'Honor your father and mother,' which is the first commandment with promise: 'that it may be well with you and you may live long on the earth.' And you, fathers, do not provoke your children to wrath, but bring them up in the training and admonition of the Lord."

When Nancie was a junior in high school, her parents had to go away on a business trip for two days. It was winter, and the weather was unpredictable. Because Nancie and her family lived thirteen miles from town, her parents told her to ride the bus to school. After her parents left, Nancie realized she had a student council meeting early the next morning before school. What could she do but drive in? It seemed the most reasonable thing to do, even

though her parents had explicitly told her not to take the car. As it happened, a heavy, wet snow had fallen in the night. On the way to school, Nancie ended up with the car teetering on the edge of a ravine. She managed to climb out of the car and hike to the highway, where she finally caught a ride with a snowplow. She arrived at school late—bedraggled and covered with mud. But she learned an important lesson about obedience that day. Obedience is a form of boundaries, of protection. Children often do not have the maturity and experience to set those safe boundaries themselves.

When our children were small, we worked hard at getting them to learn to obey us. We didn't always do so well. We made a lot of mistakes, but we tried to teach them the principle of obedience for their safety, their security, and their ultimate happiness. We also knew that when our children learn to obey us, it's easier for them to learn to obey God. We found that when we tried consistently and lovingly to require obedience, our children did respond, although some of them were more headstrong at times than others.

We had reasons we asked them to be obedient: Actions have consequences. We remember one time when we had to be away, we told our teenaged son not to have friends over to our house. We came home a few days later to find the house a mess and the neighbors upset because our son had had a party in our absence. It had gotten out of control. He was penitent, but he was also held responsible: He had to make the rounds to the neighbors to apologize, and he had to pay for the living room carpet to be cleaned.

People who've done outstanding exploits for God are just ordinary humans who've learned the secrets of obedience. Obedience to God is following His commandments and doing them: "You shall love the Lord your God with all your heart, with all your soul, with all your mind, and with all your strength. . . . You shall love your neighbor as yourself.

There is no other commandment greater than these" (Mark 12:30-31).

These are difficult areas for us as parents because we want our children to learn obedience from the heart, not just to be intimidated by harsh rules and legalism. We want our children to learn "the will of God from the heart" (Eph. 6:6). Obedience to God does not mean a decimation of our will, of who we are. It means a surrendering of our will to God's greater, wiser will. When we are able to do that, we will find obedience to God's will to be a liberating, joyful place.

I pray that my children will learn the secret strength that lies in obedience to those whom God has placed over them. But most of all, I pray that my children will know the adventurous life of obedience to God.

R E F L E C T I O N

"God never insists on our obedience; human authority does. Our Lord does not give us rules and regulations; He makes very clear what the standard is, and if the relation of my spirit to Him is that of love, I will do all He wants me to do without the slightest hesitation. If I begin to object, it is because I love someone else in competition with Him, namely, myself."

Oswald Chambers, *He Shall Glorify Me*

"The final test of love is obedience, not sweet emotions, not willingness to sacrifice, not zeal, but obedience to the commandments of Christ."

A. W. Tozer, *That Incredible Christian*

FAMILY INTERACTION

1 Have a family meeting and discuss your family's rules. Ask, "Why is it important to obey these rules?" If you need to establish some new rules, enlist everyone's help in deciding what is fair.

2 Discuss a game that you all enjoy and talk about the rules of the game. Why is it important to have rules in a game (board games, sports, etc.)?

3 Take some time to study and talk about the Ten Commandments (Exod. 20:1-17). Discuss the possible reasons God had for giving these commandments and asking His people to obey them.

4 Discuss current events (perhaps some things in the news) that are consequences of disobedience to God.

COMMUNICATING THE BLESSING

I pray for you, my child, to learn the supreme joy of obedience to God. I pray that you will understand that His ways are best, that He loves you with an everlasting love, and that you can trust Him in the smallest details of life. I pray that you will study God's Word to know His voice. And in the quiet places of your heart, may you know that He is God.

MY PRAYER FOR MY CHILD

NAME _____ DATE _____

_____

_____

FOLLOW-UP PRAYERS, ANSWERS, AND INSIGHTS

NAME _____ DATE _____

_____

_____

Obedience

LORD, HELP MY CHILD TO LEARN...

PERSISTENCE

8

Let us not become weary in doing good, for at the proper time

we will reap a harvest if we do not give up.

Galatians 6:9, NIV

P R A Y E R

Lord, how often we give in when we should persist. We are a people impatient to have what we want. We become easily bored, distracted, discouraged. Help my child to have that stick-to-it quality that helps him or her be a "conqueror" through You. Give my child the quality that Jacob had when he wrestled with You, as he declared, "I will not let You go unless You bless me" (Gen. 32:26).

S C R I P T U R E

"Ask, and it will be given to you; seek, and you will find; knock, and it will be opened to you" (Matt. 7:7).

We have been blessed with several very persistent children—especially our two youngest, Amy and Andrew. You could call them stubborn at times, I suppose. One day I overheard Andy tell Amy when she was thinking about quitting basketball, "Amy, Carmichaels aren't quitters!"

"I know, I know," she muttered, and she stuck with it.

When Andy was a toddler, he hated to stay in his bed at night. I (Nancie) remember sitting outside his bedroom door, reading James Dobson's *The Strong-Willed Child* for reinforcement. Andy's persistence has paid off though. Channeled properly, it has helped him win a spot on Little League's All-Star team, even though he was only an alternate. And it has helped him win a starting spot on his basketball team after beginning the season on the bench.

Amy has many learning disabilities, and her persistence is invaluable. Learning to do things such as tie her shoes or ride a bike has taken extra effort for her. This year, she just started seventh grade. She came home the first day convinced she could never pass math. Thanks to a positive, caring teacher—and Amy's dogged persistence—two months

later, Amy won the Student of the Month award for her grade in math.

When strong winds buffet a tree, it develops strong fiber and relies on its deep root system to withstand storms. This is how we develop fortitude, persistence, and the strength of heart that enable us to meet adversity, pain, or persecution. The psalmist David was persistent in his pursuit of God. "As the deer pants for the water brooks, so pants my soul for You, O God. My soul thirsts for God, for the living God" (Ps. 42:1-2). This is our prayer and deepest desire for our children: that they will be persistent in their pursuit of God. There is no greater challenge, no higher calling than to persist in the things of God.

A few years ago, our son Jon dated a beautiful and kind girl that seemed right for him in every way—except that she and Jon did not share the same faith. They had many intense conversations about God and doctrine, always ending at an impasse. This situation led Jon to a serious study of the Scriptures. He persisted in knowing the truth for himself. Later, he told his dad, "That is when I fell in love with God and realized I would be pursuing Him all my life."

God is certainly persistent with us: "He who began a good work in you will carry it on to completion until the day of Christ Jesus" (Phil. 1:6, NIV). He will not forsake the work of His hands (Ps. 138:8). That's us! We are the work of His hands. How comforting to know that God doesn't give up on us. We are the ones who too often give up—perhaps just before we break through to success or to achievement. The woman with a chronic problem in Mark 5:24-34 pressed through the crowd to touch the hem of Jesus' garment, and she was healed. "Pressing through" may require struggle—trying and failing, then trying again—but with the goal in mind, we can keep going. Someone once said, "We are not at our best perched at the summit; we are climbers, at our best when the way is steep." This is part of being human—the struggle to survive.

The race of life is a marathon, not a sprint. We can encourage our children to persist in going after the good things, to pursue their growth and walk with the Lord by remembering that since "we are surrounded by so great a cloud of witnesses, let us lay aside every weight, and the sin which so easily ensnares us, and let us run with endurance the race that is set before us, looking unto Jesus, the author and finisher of our faith" (Heb. 12:1-2).

I pray that my children will persist in the important things of life, that they will realize that good things sometimes come at a price, at great effort. And I especially pray that they will pursue the knowledge of the Lord.

R E F L E C T I O N

"Nothing in the world can take the place of persistence. Talent will not; nothing is more common than unsuccessful men with talent. Genius will not; unrewarded genius is almost a proverb. Education will not; the world is full of educated derelicts. Persistence and determination alone . . . will solve the problems of the human race."

Calvin Coolidge

"A great oak is only a little nut that held his ground."

L & N magazine

"Lots of people limit their possibilities by giving up easily. Never tell yourself this is too much for me. It's no use. I can't go on. If you do, you're licked, and by your own thinking, too. Keep believing and keep on keeping on."

Norman Vincent Peale, *The Power of Positive Thinking*

F A M I L Y   I N T E R A C T I O N

1 Sit with your child and each make a list of three things: short-term goals, long-term goals (education, vocation, etc.), and spiritual goals.

2 Get together and discuss ways each person intends to meet each of these goals. Discuss ways you can help each other meet the goals.

3 Encourage each other to put aside this list and come back to it later to evaluate how each of you has done at persistence.

4 Discuss with your child this question: Is persistence ever a bad thing? If so, in what situations and why?

C O M M U N I C A T I N G   T H E   B L E S S I N G

I pray for you, my child, to learn persistence. I pray that you will not give up easily when it comes to the important things of life. May you have that extra determination to hang in there to be all that God intends you to be.

MY PRAYER FOR MY CHILD

NAME _____ DATE _____

_____

_____

_____

FOLLOW-UP PRAYERS, ANSWERS, AND INSIGHTS

NAME _____ DATE _____

_____

_____

RESPONSIBILITY

9

For each one shall bear his own load.

Galatians 6:5

PRAYER

I pray that my child will grow into a responsible person—responsible in character and in behavior. O Lord, please give me, the parent, the wisdom and skill to encourage this maturation. Help me to become a responsible parent.

SCRIPTURE

"Speaking the truth in love, [we] may grow up in all things into Him who is the head—Christ" *(Eph. 4:15).*

In *The Book of Virtues* William J. Bennett writes, "Responsible persons are mature people who have taken charge of themselves and their conduct, who own their actions and own up to them—who answer for them. We help foster a mature sense of responsibility in our children in the same way that we help cultivate their other desirable traits: by practice and by example. Household chores, extracurricular activities, after-school jobs, and volunteer work all contribute to maturation if parental example and expectations are clear, consistent, and communicate with the developing powers of the child."

It seems we have a nation full of victims who complain because they can't find a job, maintain a relationship, or become a success. They blame all their woes on someone else—parents, employers, the educational system. Abigail Van Buren wrote, "If you want your children to keep their feet on the ground, put some responsibility on their shoulders."

We are not perfect parents. When Jon was in second grade, his teacher came to me (Nancie) and said, "Jon needs to learn responsibility." I had three other little boys at home, and in those days I was thinking mainly of survival—getting the laundry and meals done and keeping the peace. I met with the teacher after school and asked, "How exactly do you teach a child responsibility?" She told me she had an eighteen-year-old son and she really didn't know but would ask around and tell me. We later had a conference with another professional, and I did get some insight. These things may have been common knowledge for others, but I didn't know them. In trying to be a good mom, I had been doing too much for my children. Jon had to learn that before he could play, he had to do his chores. He had to learn that before he could have free time at recess, he needed to do his work. If there were things he could do on his own—picking out his clothes, putting things away—he should do them, not wait for me to do them.

In our desire to be good parents, I've found we often rob our children of responsibility, not allowing them to learn through experience. A few summers ago one of our sons got a brand-new used car to drive to school and work. Bill painstakingly taught him how and why to change the oil and what it meant when that red light came on. Well, the red light eventually came on, but this eager young man never had time to put in another quart of oil. So one afternoon on a lonely stretch of highway, the engine burned up. The car had to be towed, and it needed a new engine, which would cost $1400. Bill felt that our son needed to pay the bill, and he did. It took him all summer to earn the money. It was a painful lesson for all of us, but now he faithfully checks and changes the oil in his car.

A valuable part of being involved in sports programs is that our kids have had to learn discipline: In order to be a part of the team, they must be at practices (on time) and keep their grades up. Our family had a higher standard for grades than the school did, and I remember one crucial semester in junior high when one of our sons wasn't sure he would get to play. He eventually did because his love for the sport motivated him to get his grades up.

One of the early lessons of the New Testament church was "If you don't work, you don't eat." Taking responsibility builds self-esteem. Taking responsibility makes us better community members, classroom students, church members, and family members. Many people have been wounded in life by people who refused to take responsibility for their actions.

Let's practice responsibility and help our children become responsible people—in our families, in our relationship with others, and in our relationship to God.

I pray that my children will learn to take responsibility for themselves. I pray that they will realize that they must answer to God for their actions and attitudes. I pray that my children will sense that God is calling them to a life of integrity.

R E F L E C T I O N

"In our efforts to avoid the necessary pain of discipline, we miss the easy yoke and light burden. We then fall into the rending frustration of trying to do and be the Christians we know we ought to be without the necessary insight and strength that only discipline can provide."

Dallas Willard, *Spirit of the Disciplines*

"Hold yourself responsible for a higher standard than anyone else expects of you. Never excuse yourself."

Henry Ward Beecher

FAMILY INTERACTION

Conduct a who's-responsible-for-what meeting:

1 Gather the family around the table, and give each member four index cards. On each of the cards, have the following headings: "Personal Responsibilities," "Household Responsibilities," "School/Work Responsibilities," and "Spiritual Responsibilities."

2 Under each category have family members write their responsibilities. For example, under "Personal Responsibilities," list make bed, brush teeth, etc. Under "Household Responsibilities," list the designated chores for each person, making it age-appropriate. Parents must fill out the cards too. It's important for children to see the specific things for which their parents are responsible. Discuss each category and its importance as you fill out your cards.

3 Have a meeting a week later to follow up on how each person did.

COMMUNICATING THE BLESSING

Responsibility

I pray for you, my child, to develop responsibility. I pray that you will take responsibility for your own actions and not worry about the other person. I pray that you will learn the joy of acting responsibly, of choosing the right thing.

MY PRAYER FOR MY CHILD

NAME _____ DATE _____

_____

_____

FOLLOW-UP PRAYERS, ANSWERS, AND INSIGHTS

NAME _____ DATE _____

_____

_____

LORD, HELP MY CHILD TO DEVELOP . . .

Authenticity

Character

Conviction

Courage

Discernment

Faith

A Heart for Missions

A Love for God's Word

A Love for Others

Optimism

A Passion for God

Purity

A Sense of Fairness

A Spirit of Generosity

Trust

PART 2

AUTHENTICITY

10

Everything about us is bare and wide open to the all-seeing eyes of our living God;

nothing can be hidden from him to whom we must explain all that we have done.

Hebrews 4:13, TLB

PRAYER

Lord, it is a natural tendency for us to be guarded, to be careful. And yet You call us to behold You with an unveiled face, with authenticity. What a beautiful thing to see that quality in my child, Lord, to see him or her have no pretensions, to be honest with You as he or she prays a stumbling prayer or expresses doubt and sometimes anger. Help my child to see that this is very good, Father, that as he or she approaches You with authenticity, with an unveiled face, You love and change him or her.

"But we all, with unveiled face, beholding as in a mirror the glory of the Lord, are being transformed into the same image from glory to glory" (2 Cor. 3:18).

The beautiful thing about children is their transparency. They respond to life as they see it. They are authentic, unhindered by other people's expectations of them. Too soon they grow up and get complicated; they hide their immediate reactions and become careful, guarded. Jesus said, "Unless you are converted and become as little children, you will by no means enter the kingdom of heaven" (Matt. 18:3).

Our Eric has always been a transparent child: What you see is what you get. That's made for some funny and uncomfortable moments, like one Sunday night when he was five years old. Getting to church that night had been a hassle (as you can imagine with four boys under the age of eight). Bill had done his share of hollering to get everybody in the car on time. We got to church, and since Bill was on the ministerial staff, he and I were sitting in a front pew on the right. Eric and Jon sat in the front row, directly in front of the pulpit. The pastor was preaching about love and said, "Some of you fathers act all lovey-dovey when you get to church; then as soon as you get in the car, you start yelling at your kids!"

In agreement with what the pastor had said, Eric stood up and shook his finger at his dad. The whole place erupted into laughter at Bill's expense, and Bill whispered in my ear with a smile pasted on his face, "I'm going to kill that kid!"

That was a good reminder to us, though, about authenticity. Who we are is far more important than what we say. Richard Foster wrote in *A Celebration of Discipline,* "The discipline of confession brings an end to pretense. God is calling into being a church that can openly confess its frail humanity and knows the forgiving and empowering graces of Christ. Honesty leads to confession, and confession leads to change."

In our relationship with God, it is essential to be honest about ourselves. Make no mistake—this can be painful. The heart can be deceitfully wicked. When we begin to take things "into our own tents" against God's Word, these things can defeat us. We take things into our lives to pacify the hurt, to cover it up. This is how addictions are formed. We don't deal with the real root of our sinful humanity and refuse to see what our wounds are doing to us and those who love us. Some people call it denial.

But when we can open ourselves up to the Great Physician and say, "Do with me what you will. I come just as I am," He does meet us.

This has not been an easy thing for us as a family to learn, but we are committed to learning it. James Dobson wrote in *Preparing for Adolescence*, "Nothing can be hidden from God, because He sees everything." We do know God sees all; it's just that we tend to want to look better to others than we actually are! But we're seeing that walking with an awareness of our humanity and acknowledging our shortcomings actually makes us stronger and more compassionate. We can truly administer God's grace when we experience it ourselves.

I pray that my children will keep an authentic, childlike quality of transparency toward themselves, others, and God. And as they look to God with an unveiled face, may their lives reflect His glory.

R E F L E C T I O N

"We must lay before him what is in us, not what ought to be in us."

C. S. Lewis

"Each of us is a person, with individual masks, scars, celebrations, moments of reflecting God, and experiences of conversion. Our prayers must spring from the indigenous souls of our own personal confrontation with the Spirit of God in our lives."

Malcolm Boyd

*"Give me a pure heart—that I may see Thee
A humble heart—that I may hear Thee
A heart of love—that I may serve Thee
A heart of faith—that I may abide with Thee."*

Dag Hammarskjöld, *Markings*

FAMILY INTERACTION

1 Read the story of Achan in Joshua 7. Discuss as a family the consequences of Achan's deceit. What can we learn from it?

2 How is it possible that we can in our humanity stand before an awesome, holy God? (Heb. 4:14-16).

3 Discuss with your child how you can make your home a safe place where both of you can practice authenticity.

COMMUNICATING THE BLESSING

I pray for you, my child, to develop authenticity, to keep an unveiled face toward God. I pray that you will let Him in more and more to the very core of your being and that you will respond to His love and His grace. I pray that you will become a mirror of His grace and reflect His glory to others.

MY PRAYER FOR MY CHILD

NAME _____ DATE _____

_____

_____

_____

FOLLOW-UP PRAYERS, ANSWERS, AND INSIGHTS

NAME _____ DATE _____

_____

_____

_____

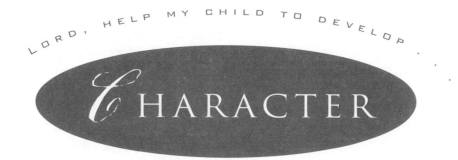

LORD, HELP MY CHILD TO DEVELOP . . .

CHARACTER

Whatever you do, work at it with all your heart, as working for the Lord, not for men.

Colossians 3:23, NIV

PRAYER

Lord, in listening to the success experts of our day, I hear all kinds of advice on how to improve the outer person: appearance, wealth, charisma, impression, authority, recognition. Few words are addressed to the inner person: the heart and the soul. I pray that my child will be shaped from the inside out rather than the outside in. Give my child holy backbone.

SCRIPTURE

"And now, my daughter, don't be afraid. I will do for you all you ask. All my fellow townsmen know that you are a woman of noble character" (Ruth 3:11, NIV).

D. L. Moody once told his son, "Character is what you are in the dark." A person of character decides what is right to do and sticks to it, *regardless*. People of character are the salt of the earth, the ones who hold families, churches, communities, and nations together. Through their moral courage, people with strong character have changed the course of things. Winston Churchill told his countrymen in the face of defeat by Germany in World War II: "Never give in, never give in, never, never, never, never." In the Bible, we see the life of Daniel, who held to his principles in a pagan land and remained a man of prayer. We see Esther, who went in before the king to intercede for her people and ultimately saved them from destruction.

It is the *regardless* that is the key to developing character. Character is doing the right thing because it is right, regardless of adversity, regardless of pressure to compromise in the midst of our daily choices. As Maltie Babcock wrote, "Good habits are not made on birthdays, nor Christian character at the new year. The workshop of character is everyday life. The uneventful and commonplace hour is where the battle is lost or won."

Eric Liddell, the flying Scotsman whose story is told in the movie *Chariots of Fire,* was a runner who qualified for the 1924 Olympics in Paris. When he learned a few months before the games that the preliminary heats were to be held on Sunday, he decided he would not run in them. For him, Sunday was the Lord's day, a day of rest, not of play. He faced a storm of criticism and was called a traitor to his country. However, Liddell did not budge. Refusing to run the 100-meter dash, which would mean competing on Sunday, he entered the 200-meter dash, placed, and won a gold medal for Great Britain, setting a new world record in the process. Eric Liddell's real legacy is standing for what he believed to be right, *regardless*. Later in life, he went to China as a missionary. He died there in a prison camp in February 1945, still doing the right thing, *regardless*.

I (Bill) recall as a child how my parents tithed to the Lord's work regardless of their circumstances, even when my father was unable to work because of a construction accident. God took care of every one of our family's needs. I saw that demonstration of character in my parents. They did the right thing in spite of adversity, in spite of the temptation to do what was convenient. Romans 5:3-4 says, "We also glory in tribulations, knowing that tribulation produces perseverance; and perseverance, character; and character, hope."

It is this very determination to stick to principle that makes a person strong, like the trees that grow near the timberline and face the strongest winds. They become—like people of character—sturdy, beautiful, and strong over time.

I pray that my children will develop character, knowing that character development is a lifetime process. I pray that they will have the moral courage to follow God, regardless of adversity.

R E F L E C T I O N

"It is with trifles, and when he is off guard, that a man reveals his character."

Arthur Schopenhauer

*"Children who grow up with their fathers do far better—emotionally, educationally, physically, every way we can measure—than children who do not. . . .
The simple truth is that fathers are irreplaceable in shaping the competence and character of their children."*

David Blankenhorn, president of the Institute for American Values

"Needed: A new 'culture of character' based on the values, traditions, and institutions that were originally the centerpiece of our society."

Rolf Zettersten, *Train Up a Child*

F A M I L Y   I N T E R A C T I O N

1 Tell your child to pick out his or her two favorite characters from a book, movie, or television show. Ask your child to explain why he or she likes these characters. Discuss the traits that make these characters who they are and what they are. Then explain to your child that the word *character* means who a person is and what that person becomes. Ask your child, "What character traits do you want in your friends?" "What character traits do you want in yourself?" "What character traits does God want in you?"

2 Pick out two contrasting characters in the Bible, such as Saul and David (1 Sam. 19–20 and 24–26) or Daniel and his accusers (Dan. 6). Discuss what character traits made them different and which traits were pleasing to God.

COMMUNICATING THE BLESSING

I pray for you, my child, to develop character. I pray that when people speak of you, they will say, "He [or she] has character," rather than, "He's [she's] a character!" And I hope that you remember that character progress is measured not in front of a crowd but when no one else is looking.

MY PRAYER FOR MY CHILD

NAME _____ DATE _____

_____

_____

_____

_____

_____

_____

Character

FOLLOW-UP PRAYERS, ANSWERS, AND INSIGHTS

NAME _____ DATE _____

_____

_____

_____

_____

_____

_____

LORD, HELP MY CHILD TO DEVELOP...

CONVICTION

My son, if sinners entice you, do not give in to them.

Proverbs 1:10, NIV

PRAYER

Conviction is essential to knowing You, Lord. Help my child to develop fixed and strong beliefs about the principles of Your Word, and help my child to feel conviction when he or she trespasses against those principles. Give my child the courage to stand up for his or her convictions in spite of criticism or current trends. And please, Lord, give my child the discernment to know the difference between the essential principles of Your eternal Word and the legalistic doctrines of the day.

SCRIPTURE

"But let your 'Yes' be 'Yes,' and your 'No,' 'No.' For whatever is more than these is from the evil one" (Matt. 5:37).

49

Esther Ahn Kim, a young Korean teacher, refused to worship at the Shinto shrines when forced to do so by the Japanese during World War II. Her stance: "If I perish, I perish." She was convinced that she must obey God at all costs. In spite of years of imprisonment and cruelty in a Japanese prison camp, she remained true to her convictions and won many fellow prisoners to Christ by her example. Her story is widely popular in Korea and Japan, and Japanese Christians have produced a film about her life. Her simple conviction that she could not worship any god other than the Lord Jesus Christ has had a lasting impact.

Today more than ever, we need a fresh wind of the Holy Spirit to convict us of sin and empower us to walk a holy life. The lines today are too often blurry as to what is right and what is wrong. Suppose the enemy wanted to capture the hearts and minds of an entire generation. How would he do it? In this invasive culture, our children are vulnerable. Movies, music, and interactive media are the language of our youth.

We parents can be living under the same roof with our children and yet be part of an entirely different culture: We listen to our Christian music and programming while our children listen to music and movies that tear down God's holy law and promote despair, hopelessness, and violence. If we are not vigilant, we can live like people from two different cultures under one roof.

How important it is for our children to know God's truth, to be strengthened by the Holy Spirit to live out that truth.

In our son Chris's public high school social studies class, the class discussed the term *born again*. The teacher asked how many in the class were born again. Chris said he raised his hand, only to find he was the only one in a large classroom. Simply raising a hand to say, "I am a follower of Jesus Christ" took conviction. Bowing our heads in prayer over a meal in a public place takes conviction. Refusing to gossip when it would be easy to do so takes conviction.

Conviction is more than just a rigid mind-set. Conviction is an overwhelming belief that *this is right* because God says it is so. Psalm 19:8-10 gives this beautiful description of the innate strength and beauty found in living with convictions:

> *The statutes of the Lord are right, rejoicing
>   the heart;*
> *The commandment of the Lord is pure,
>   enlightening the eyes;*
> *The fear of the Lord is clean, enduring forever;*

Conviction

The judgments of the Lord are true and
righteous altogether.
More to be desired are they than gold,
Yea, than much fine gold;
Sweeter also than honey and the honeycomb.

God's Spirit helps us to do what is right,
impressing on us that above all else, we must
obey Him with a whole heart, with single-
minded purpose. We must do what is right not
out of guilt but because God's ways are right.

I pray that my children will have a fresh understand-
ing of conviction, that they will be so convinced of
God's truth, so in awe of His ways, so in love with
His purity that they will stand for righteousness.

R E F L E C T I O N

"We ought to recognize one of the great problems in our modern Christianity:
Those who come to Christ probably have their minds made up that to stay
sane they must remain 'adjusted' to society around them.
"This notion has been drilled into them from their playpen, and it never occurs
to them to question it. There is a 'norm' out there somewhere to which they
must conform, and that norm is above criticism. Their success and
happiness depend upon how well they adjust to it; and Christianity,
though it may add something to it, must never disagree with the main idea!
"This is the popular notion in the world: 'To be happy, adjust to the social norm!'
The problem is that the idea will not hold up under examination.
The world does not know where it is going; it has not found life's highest good.
It is instead puzzled, frightened, and frustrated.
"Thankfully, it was to this kind of world Jesus came. He died for its sin
and now lives for the salvation of all who repudiate it!"

A. W. Tozer, *Renewed Day by Day*

"The battle is lost or won in the secret places of the will before God, never first in
the eternal world. The Spirit of God apprehends me, and I am obliged to get alone
with God and fight the battle out before Him. . . . Every now and then . . .
God brings us to . . . the Great Divide in life; from that point we either go
towards a more and more dilatory and useless type of Christian life,
or we become more and more ablaze for the glory of God."

Oswald Chambers, *My Utmost for His Highest*

Conviction

FAMILY INTERACTION

1 Discuss some of the social ills your child may see regularly at school, in the neighborhood, or on television: drugs, alcohol, immorality, cheating, lying, violence, crime. Ask your child to explain why these behaviors are wrong. Help your child to understand that what he or she says about these behaviors reflects his or her convictions. Talk about your family convictions and why we need to stand firm on what we believe.

2 Read together several stories that illustrate people who stood up for their convictions. Discuss how the person's convictions enabled him or her to do what was right. If you have a hard time finding stories, see William J. Bennett's *The Book of Virtues*.

COMMUNICATING THE BLESSING

I pray for you, my child, to develop and respond to conviction. I pray that you will have fixed and strong beliefs that God exists, that His Word is unalterably true, that He loves you unconditionally, and that He expects you to love other people as He does. I hope that you will stand up for these truths, no matter what.

MY PRAYER FOR MY CHILD

NAME _____ DATE _____

_____

_____

_____

FOLLOW-UP PRAYERS, ANSWERS, AND INSIGHTS

NAME _____ DATE _____

_____

_____

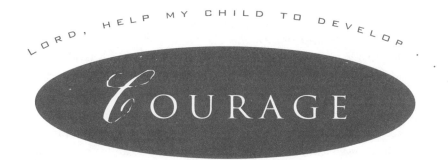

LORD, HELP MY CHILD TO DEVELOP . . .

COURAGE

We are his house, if we hold on to our courage

and the hope of which we boast.

Hebrews 3:6, NIV

13

P R A Y E R

Lord, today many of us retreat rather than face hardship or criticism. We often shrink from challenges You've called us to face. Help my child to stand in times when others may shrink or fall away. Give my child the kind of courage the three Hebrew young men displayed when they faced the fiery furnace rather than bow down to a false god. Give my child the kind of courage that David had when he faced the lion, the bear, and ultimately the giant. Most of all, give my child courage to dare to believe You.

"Be on your guard; stand firm in the faith; be men of courage; be strong" (1 Cor. 16:13, NIV).

Courage

The definition of *courage* is "the state or quality of mind or spirit that enables one to face danger with confidence and resolution; bravery." Courage comes when we realize where our strength lies. Courage is not necessarily a strong sense of self-reliance but a belief that as we are obedient to God, *He will make a way where there is no way.* It is being confident that doing the right thing is worth the risk of danger.

David was able to defeat the lion, the bear, Goliath, and hostile armies because he confessed, "Lord, You are my strength." Queen Esther was able to confront the king, risking her life to save her people, because she had the quiet confidence that this was the only right thing to do. Her attitude was "If I perish, I perish."

Sometimes it takes courage just to keep going, to get up to face another day. It takes courage for Andy to keep trying in his second-year algebra class, not to give up, but to press on when he would like to quit. It takes courage for us parents to allow our children to start driving cars or just to take the next step in life.

To live with courage is to face our own fear, to say, "The Lord is God! What can other people do to me?" On the day of our sons' really important games, when a lot was at stake, we would quote to them from Psalm 18:29, "For by You I can run against a troop, by my God I can leap over a wall."

When our children face new challenges—trying out for a sport, playing in a concert, performing in a school play, or just finding a new friend—and are paralyzed by fear, we can encourage them to do all things through Christ, who strengthens them.

Daniel and the three Hebrew young men had the courage to follow their convictions in matters of conscience, such as what they should eat and drink as well as the more consuming, all-important choice, whom to worship—even in extreme adversity.

When our son Chris was a senior in high school, he faced a test of courage. At a school function on the beach, several of the kids managed to procure some cases of beer when the chaperones were distracted. Chris faced a dilemma: Should he tell the authorities and risk being ostracized by his peers, or should he join in the fun and be one of the gang? To his credit, he didn't drink with his friends; instead, he stood for what he knew to be the right decision. But he didn't tell on them either, choosing rather to express concern that what they were doing was wrong and that their drinking would be discovered. Sure enough, they were soon found out and sent home.

As I look back on that incident, I wish we as his parents had affirmed his courage for not drinking with the rest; instead, we were outraged that the beer party even happened, not fully understanding his predicament. Thankfully, Chris had the courage to live out his convictions, and we respect him for that. It takes courage to go against the grain. Deuteronomy 31:6 gives the charge: "Be strong and of good courage, do not fear nor be afraid of them; for the Lord your God, He is the One who goes with you. He will not leave you nor forsake you." We have courage when we are convinced that we are not alone.

We all urgently need courage to live with integrity and faith. How we need courage to grow, to be all that we can be, to live for God.

I pray that my children will have courage, that they will face their fears and step out to new challenges, trusting in God because He promises to be with them always.

R E F L E C T I O N

"Criticism challenges it—adventure arouses it—danger incites it— threats quicken it. COURAGE—another word for inner strength, presence of mind against odds, determination to hang in there to venture, persevere, withstand hardship."

Charles Swindoll, *Growing Strong in the Seasons of Life*

"We grow spiritually by obeying God through the words of Jesus being made spirit and life to us, and by paying attention to where we are, not to whether we are growing or not. We grow spiritually as our Lord grew physically, by a life of simple, unobtrusive obedience."

Oswald Chambers, *My Utmost for His Highest*

"Do not pray for easy lives. Pray to be stronger men! Do not pray for tasks equal to your powers. Pray for powers equal to your tasks."

Phillips Brooks

FAMILY INTERACTION

1 Read and tell the story of Daniel (Dan. 1–6).

2 Ask your child these questions: "How do we develop courage?" "Why is courage important?" "Where do you need courage the most?"

3 Describe a situation in which your child will need courage: "If you were with your friends and they were about to do something you knew was wrong (cheat on a test, tell a lie, do a mean thing to another child, drink at a party, use drugs), how would you respond?"

4 Ask your child, "How may I pray specifically for you to have courage? Do you need courage at school, at a sports activity, with friends, at work, in making choices?"

COMMUNICATING THE BLESSING

I pray for you, my child, to develop courage. I pray that God will grant you courage to stand up for what is right, just, holy, and true. As you dare to trust Him, God will be with you, and you will be strong in His power and might.

MY PRAYER FOR MY CHILD

NAME _____ DATE _____

_____

_____

FOLLOW-UP PRAYERS, ANSWERS, AND INSIGHTS

NAME _____ DATE _____

_____

_____

LORD, HELP MY CHILD TO DEVELOP . . .

*D*ISCERNMENT

14

I am your servant; give me discernment that I may understand your statutes. . . .

Because I love your commands more than gold, more than pure gold,

and because I consider all your precepts right, I hate every wrong path.

Psalm 119:125, 127-128, NIV

P R A Y E R

More than ever, Lord, words seem deceptive. *Personal values* now means "living as I please." *Abortion* is called "a woman's right to choose." *Suicide* is called "self-deliverance." *Homosexuality* is termed "sexual preference," and *fornication* is simply "expressing love." I pray You will help my child see through words and labels to discern right from wrong.

"My son, if you receive my words, and treasure my commands within you, so that you incline your ear to wisdom, and apply your heart to understanding; yes, if you cry out for discernment, and lift up your voice for understanding, if you seek her as silver, and search for her as for hidden treasures; then you will understand the fear of the Lord, and find the knowledge of God" (Prov. 2:1-5).

I N S I G H T

We all need discernment, that ability to weigh all the facts and then choose the right thing, the decision that would lead to God's best for us and for other people. Discernment is more than just knowledge, even more than wisdom. The story of King Solomon shows a man to whom God gave great gifts of wisdom, yet Solomon chose to override his discernment with his own selfish desires (1 Kings 11:6). Solomon compromised by accommodating his wives and their idol worship, which led him away from God.

Discernment involves listening between the lines, seeing the real agenda, and responding in a balanced way. Discernment is *response* not *reaction*. *Discernment* means not making snap judgments. It is considering what is going on inside of us. *Discernment* means asking our Father for supernatural wisdom in a matter, then responding, regardless of pressure to do otherwise.

Teaching children discernment usually will require taking away parental instructions and allowing them to think through a decision for themselves.

Before our oldest son, Jon, was married recently, his younger brother Eric, who was to be Jon's best man, and several of their friends began planning a bachelor party. If you know anything about the traditions of bachelor parties, you know that they can get pretty wild. During the planning session, several of my son's friends (not all of whom are professing Christians) got caught up with what they should do. One thing led to another, until the plans were wild enough to make Eric uneasy.

Seeking some discernment, Eric called me (Bill) and said, "Dad, if I go with what the guys want to do, it will no doubt create some compromising situations. On one hand, I don't want to disappoint the guys. On the other hand, I don't want to do anything that we will regret later. Besides that, my two younger brothers will be coming, and I am worried about what influence this will have on them."

Discernment

Eric, always the generous one, went on to explain that on impulse he had already put down a $100 nonrefundable deposit at the establishment where this party was to take place.

I listened as he vacillated, weighing the pros and cons, wrestling between pleasing his friends and keeping his convictions. I sensed this was a crossroads in Eric's life. Finally, I said, "Son, I can't answer this one for you. You have to make this decision for yourself. I believe there is a lot of wisdom already in your heart, and God will give you discernment if you are willing to listen. I think God is already speaking to you, or you wouldn't have made this call. I will be praying for you."

The next afternoon I received another call from Eric. "Dad, I've decided to cancel the party as planned. I lost $100, and some of the guys were disappointed, but I know I'm doing the right thing. I decided to have a softball and pizza party instead."

Whew! I thought, as a grin spread across my face. "Eric, I am so proud of you. I know this was not an easy decision. I know that taking a stand can be embarrassing. Conviction is often interpreted as intolerance. Following wisdom doesn't get you invited back to the party very often. I know that people your age are not standing in line to follow a man of discernment. But in the long term, if you choose what's right in God's sight, you will be standing when others have fallen."

I pray that my children will seek to have discernment in their lives. I pray that they will want to know what is really going on, that they will have the courage to be discerning toward themselves and others, and that they will walk with integrity before God.

Discernment

R E F L E C T I O N

"Discernment will act as a watchdog to keep us from getting lost in the morass of tomorrow's depravity and deception even as we keep pace with its advancements."

Charles Swindoll, *Rise and Shine*

"O God and Father, I repent of my sinful preoccupation with visible things. The world has been too much with me. You have been here, and I knew it not. I have been blind to Your presence. Open my eyes that I may behold You in and around me. For Christ's sake, Amen."

A. W. Tozer, *The Pursuit of God*

FAMILY INTERACTION

1 Ask your child, "What does *discernment* mean?" (The dictionary suggests that discernment involves the ability to separate out the issues and distinguish between various options. Sometimes it involves using more than our senses to detect the truth—hearing God's will with our heart.)

2 Describe a situation in which you saw your child use discernment. Affirm your child for his or her ability to see right from wrong and then decide to do the right thing.

3 What things can distort our ability to discern?

4 Why is discernment necessary these days?

COMMUNICATING THE BLESSING

I pray for you, my child, to develop discernment. I pray that you will be able to avoid dressing up immorality with nicer-sounding phrases to justify what is wrong. I pray that you will see and choose to do what is right.

MY PRAYER FOR MY CHILD

NAME _____ DATE _____

_____

_____

_____

FOLLOW-UP PRAYERS, ANSWERS, AND INSIGHTS

NAME _____ DATE _____

_____

_____

_____

LORD, HELP MY CHILD TO DEVELOP . . .

FAITH

15

Without faith it is impossible to please Him, for he who comes to God must believe

that He is, and that He is a rewarder of those who diligently seek Him.

Hebrews 11:6

PRAYER

Lord, Your Word says that faith comes by hearing the Word. Help me be faithful in teaching Your Word to my children so that faith may come alive in them. Help them believe that Your Word and its promises are true, that Jesus is alive, that by Your power difficulties can be overcome, that disease can be conquered, that mountains can be moved, and that the human spirit can be gloriously changed.

SCRIPTURE

"For by grace you have been saved through faith, and that not of yourselves; it is the gift of God" (Eph. 2:8).

Faith

Families are prime places to learn faith. How else can you explain the mysteries of marriage, of carving out a living, of daring to have children and send them into the world? How else can you explain a life yielded to God, daring to dream new ventures with Him? Faith is God's miraculous, intangible, priceless gift that gives us courage to believe Him, accept His Word as truth, and trust Him with our future.

Last May we were back at our alma mater for our son Eric's graduation. As we looked at the large gathering of people on the Commons and watched another of our sons walk across the platform into the world, we remembered a young couple in love with life and each other and unlimited dreams. If we could, we would say to that couple, "You say your number one desire is to follow God wholeheartedly. That's good. But there is no way to describe the conflicts that will burn inside you as you take on the challenge of this faith walk. You will face career choices, spiritual choices, choices at every crossroad. You can't see the giants in the Promised Land you so eagerly embrace. Now your giants are finances and opportunity. But the real obstacles to faith are not as obvious. They are inside you: negative attitudes, self-centeredness, pride, low self-esteem, the desire for security. But as you wage a lifelong quest to conquer them, you will grow in faith."

Of course, we were that young couple. But we are learning that the lessons of faith never stop. God will take us only as far as we are willing to go with Him, and then He waits patiently for us to take the next step. Paul encouraged Timothy, "Fight the good fight, holding on to faith and a good conscience. Some have rejected these and so have shipwrecked their faith" (1 Tim. 1:18-19, NIV).

We tell the stories of faith to our children, the stories of how our parents and grandparents went through deep waters, the stories of how God was there with them, and the stories of how God has tested and nurtured our own faith in difficult circumstances. I (Bill) have tried to tell our children what it was like when I was a boy in Colorado and my father had a serious accident and was unable to support the family. Never was our faith tested as it was then, as we trusted God for just the basics of life. And God provided in miraculous ways. We learned lessons of faith during that time as never before. As we tell these stories of God's faithfulness, we pray that our children will exercise the measure of faith that they do have and so grow in faith.

I pray that my children will develop faith and will know God's faithfulness as they have the courage to step into the unknown, knowing God is there with them.

R E F L E C T I O N

"Faith is not belief without proof, but trust without reservation."

Elton Trueblood

*"I would much prefer to live my life on the sharp, cutting edge of
reality than dreaming on the soft, phony mattress of fantasy.
Reality is the tempered poker that keeps the fires alive—
it's the spark that prompts the engine to keep running."*

Charles Swindoll, *Growing Strong in the Seasons of Life*

*"O God, in all ages you have imparted yourself to man and set alight the fire of
faith in his heart, grant to me the faith which comes from search.
Cleanse my life from all that negates and crushes out faith,
and fill it with the purity and honesty which foster it. Cleanse me
from the evil which makes unbelief its friend, and drive it far from me,
so that, being willing in all things to do your will, I may know the truth
which shall set me free. Through Jesus Christ, our Lord. Amen."*

Samuel M. Shoemaker, *Daily Prayer Companion*

F A M I L Y I N T E R A C T I O N

1 Share a childhood story in which you had to trust God, by faith, to give the answer or meet a need. Ask your child to share a story of faith from his or her life. If your child is unable to do that, tell him or her a story in which you perceived that he or she acted in faith, believing that God would answer. Affirm your child's expression of faith in that instance.

2 Look up the characters in Hebrews 11: Faith's Hall of Fame. Note that many of them were imperfect people (Moses murdered; David committed adultery; Rahab was a prostitute). They were ordinary people who came to trust God and did great things. Discuss these people with your children. Let them see that having faith doesn't mean we are perfect but that we take what we have, rely on God, and let Him do it through us.

COMMUNICATING THE BLESSING

I pray for you, my child, that God will give you the gift of faith to believe in Him. I pray that you will cling in faith to Him in times of doubt or fear or uncertainty. I pray that in exercising your faith you will know that His Word is true.

MY PRAYER FOR MY CHILD

NAME _____ DATE _____

_____

_____

_____

_____

_____

_____

Faith

FOLLOW-UP PRAYERS, ANSWERS, AND INSIGHTS

NAME _____ DATE _____

_____

_____

_____

_____

_____

_____

LORD, HELP MY CHILD TO DEVELOP A HEART FOR . . .

*M*ISSIONS

16

The harvest is plentiful but the workers are few. Ask the Lord of the harvest,

therefore, to send out workers into his harvest field.

Matthew 9:37-38, NIV

P R A Y E R

Lord, let my child see the lost world as Your harvest field. Give my child a burden and a zeal to be one of Your harvest workers. And whether Your call is to a foreign country, the inner city, the office, the home, or any other place, may my child look at the field and find his or her place as a harvester in it.

S C R I P T U R E

"Go into all the world and preach the gospel to every creature. He who believes and is baptized will be saved; but he who does not believe will be condemned" (Mark 16:15-16).

The world is becoming smaller. Since the great thrusts of the London Missionary Society and the China Inland Mission, the world has changed. The needs are as great as ever, however, and the lost are just as lost. America's face is changing as immigrants pour in and as Muslim and Buddhist groups are on America's doorstep.

As never before, we need a new vision of the lost. We must dream and pray for new ways to reach our world. We have at our disposal education and technology, but we must pray for a heart for missions, echoing the words of Bob Pierce, founder of World Vision: "Let my heart be broken with the things that break the heart of God."

We need men like Dr. David Livingstone, who was convinced that if he found the source of the Nile, he would have the political credibility and clout to influence the stop of slave trading that was decimating Africa; and he did. We need women like Catherine Booth, who saw the devastating effects of unemployment and alcohol on families and waded in there with the gospel in one hand and practical help in the other. She and her husband, William, have had a lasting impact on our world today through the great work of the Salvation Army.

Both Bill and I (Nancie) had parents with missionary hearts. They took us to missionary services, invited missionaries to stay in our homes, and led our families in praying for missionaries. Missionaries were our heroes, who embodied commitment and sacrifice. Through our parents' example, we realize the importance of exposing our children to missions. It's taken a lot of diligence and discernment because with the invasive media of the day, it's easy to become calloused to the needs around us. We've seen that it's most effective to bring our children into our own missionary vision. We pray for and financially support specific missionaries. At times we have sponsored a child in one of the many programs offered, and we keep the child's photo on our refrigerator as a reminder. We've also seen that it's effective to involve our children in practical and local ministries, such as helping in children's church.

Perhaps the most powerful way for our children to have a missionary heart is for them to go on a missions trip or to be involved in ministries that reach people who need Jesus. Our son Jon has gone on several mission outreaches to Mexico with our church and through his college. When he was a college freshman, he went with his school to Indonesia. Chris, another of our sons, went on a missions trip to Mexico to work with families that lived in the city dump. Eric was part of a basketball team that worked with disadvantaged kids in the city. Our son Andy is planning a missions trip this summer. These hands-on experiences of getting out there and touching lives for Jesus change us because we see the needs in a vivid way and we see how the gospel of Jesus Christ makes a difference. We in the developed world have been blessed by much, but touching those who are poor and needy brings a special touch of God on our lives and increases our vision. We are also humbled by seeing that God has "chosen the poor of this world to be rich in faith and heirs of the kingdom" (James 2:5).

Even if we cannot go to a foreign country, we can find needs all around us. Our own home state of Oregon has one of the highest rates of non–church attendance and has just passed the first physician-assisted suicide law, which thanks to a courageous judge, has been blocked for now. How can we be heard by such a world?

We know certain things: The human heart has not changed, and Jesus never changes. So we pray for hungry hearts to seek Him and for fresh, innovative ways to tell the never-changing Story. The first prerequisite to having a missionary heart is to see the need. Jesus said, "Lift up your eyes and look at the fields, for they are already white for harvest!" (John 4:35).

I pray that my children will have missionary hearts, that they will give freely of themselves and their substance. Give me strength as a parent to release my children to the cause of Christ. I pray that we will not be overwhelmed by all the needs but that we will be moved with compassion as Christ was, seeing the "one lost sheep."

R E F L E C T I O N

*"Sometimes avalanches have been started by a skier just shouting a few words.
It only needs a small amount of snow to be disturbed by that shout,
and soon thousands of tons of snow will be thundering down the mountainside.
In the same way a few words spoken to God our Father in Jesus' name can set off
an 'avalanche' of God's power in any part of the world.
Even when we think our prayers are small and weak, God can use them
if we trust in Him, because He is so powerful."*

Jill Johnstone, *You Can Change the World*

*"The Spirit of Christ is the spirit of missions, and the nearer we get to Him, the
more intensely missionary we must become."*

Henry Martyn

FAMILY INTERACTION

1 Ask your child, "Have you ever been lost? What was it like to be found?" Ask your child, "What does it mean to be spiritually lost?"

2 Read as a family Matthew 9:36-38, and discuss what Christ's compassion means and how it should change how we see the lost.

3 Choose a country or ethnic group that you would like to learn about. Read about that country or group. Find out what percentage of that country or ethnic group is Christian. If you live in a large city, visit an ethnic neighborhood that reflects the country or group you are exploring. Pray for the people in that country or ethnic group and for the people who will tell them about Jesus.

COMMUNICATING THE BLESSING

I pray for you, my child, to develop a missionary heart. Wherever God calls you, I pray that you will be an active part of the great commission to share the Good News of the gospel of Jesus Christ.

Missions

MY PRAYER FOR MY CHILD

NAME _____ DATE _____

_____

_____

_____

FOLLOW-UP PRAYERS, ANSWERS, AND INSIGHTS

NAME _____ DATE _____

_____

_____

_____

GOD'S WORD

17

Nothing is perfect except your words. Oh, how I love them. I think about them all day long. They make me wiser than my enemies because they are my constant guide.

Psalm 119:96-98, TLB

PRAYER

O God, help me to influence my child with a love for Your holy Word. Let the Scripture come alive. Let it be more than stories and legend. Let it be Your living breath, Your very voice to my child. Give my child the capacity to hide Your Word in his or her heart so that when difficult circumstances occur, my child will be able to find Your Word.

SCRIPTURE

"I have not departed from the commandment of His lips; I have treasured the words of His mouth more than my necessary food" (Job 23:12).

We were on a family vacation, boating near the San Juan Islands off the Washington coast when we got caught in a gale storm. Things went from bad to worse when we developed engine trouble. Scared and helpless, we watched the wind blowing us toward jagged rocks as we rushed about putting on life jackets. Then advice came over our CB: "Put down your anchor!" Feeling sheepish that we hadn't thought of it, we immediately dropped anchor and were secure until help came.

God's Word is an anchor to us in these tumultuous times. It is a bedrock foundation to our lives. In the Bible, God offers direction, comfort, correction, and instruction in righteousness (2 Tim. 3:16). In the Bible, God reveals Jesus to us: "And the Word became flesh and dwelt among us, and we beheld His glory, the glory as of the only begotten of the Father, full of grace and truth" (John 1:14).

How do we convey this truth to our children?

One of my (Nancie's) earliest memories of Sunday school was being in the beginners class. My teacher, Mrs. Kimball, had made a big box that looked like a Bible. Covered with construction paper and gold lettering, it had a lid that came off. Inside the box she had special treats that she dispensed as rewards for

reciting Scripture verses we had memorized. That was the humble beginning of an awe-filled reverence and desire to dig out the "good" things that are in the Bible.

As early as we can remember, God's Word has been held in the highest respect. We stood in church services as the Word was read. Our parents read the Scripture to us during family devotions. We watched our parents read the Bible on their own, soaking in the words. In a myriad of ways, we were given the idea that inside God's Word are many wonderful treasures; we had only to dig them out.

When I (Bill) graduated from high school, my older sister and brother-in-law gave me a Bible. In the flyleaf, my sister quoted, "Only one life, 'twill soon be past. Only what's done for Christ will last." That was well over thirty years ago, but that Bible is as relevant to me as it ever was, as it has been to countless people through the ages. God's Word is the plumb line, the measuring stick for our lives.

Reformer John Knox, considered the founder of the Presbyterian Church in Scotland, had the moral courage to defend the cause of Christ against queens, kings, and others. He is credited with the prayer, "Give me Scotland or I die!" Born in 1505, Knox grew in his intellectual thirst, and that thirst led him to the works of Jerome and Augustine and eventually to a critical and thorough study of the Bible. Knox lived by this principle: Nothing is lawful in the church which is not found in the Word of God. He was tireless in his study of the Bible, reading it through each month, almost until the day of his death. He wrote, "Dear brethren . . . exercise yourselves in the book of the Lord your God. Let no day slip over without some comfort received from the mouth of God. Open your ears, and He will speak even pleasant things to your heart. . . . Above all things, dear brethren, study to practice in life that which the Word of God commandeth, and then be assured that ye shall never hear nor read the same without fruit."

Today, with TV, VCRs, and interactive media, our children's minds and hearts are being bombarded on every level. It is a tremendous challenge to us parents to encourage our children to read, to learn, to love God's Word. But through prayer, through diligence, through modeling, and through personal discipline, it can be done. Only through the truth of God's Word can we and our children experience a fresh "reformation" to live out God's Word in our lives.

I pray that my children will seek to know the truth of God's Word for themselves and that this knowledge will lead them to the fear of the Lord because that reverence is the beginning of wisdom.

R E F L E C T I O N

"Self-control, human kindness, respect, and peacefulness can be manifested . . . if we will return to this ultimate resource, the Bible, in our homes and schools."
James Dobson, *Dr. Dobson Answers Your Questions*

"A thorough knowledge of the Bible is worth more than a college education."
Theodore Roosevelt

"Nobody ever outgrows Scripture; the book widens and deepens with our years."
Charles H. Spurgeon

F A M I L Y   I N T E R A C T I O N

1 Help your child memorize the names of the books of the Old and New Testaments.

2 Ask your child to find a favorite Scripture verse to share with the rest of the family at a mealtime.

3 Spend time looking up verses that refer to God's Word (such as Ps. 119:105), and discuss with your child what the verses mean.

C O M M U N I C A T I N G   T H E   B L E S S I N G

I pray for you, my child, to develop a love for God's Word. May you find in the pages of God's Word the greatest adventure, mystery, and love story ever written. And may you forever find His Word to be the source of all the answers you will need in this life and for the life to come.

MY PRAYER FOR MY CHILD

NAME _____ DATE _____

_____

_____

_____

_____

FOLLOW-UP PRAYERS, ANSWERS, AND INSIGHTS

NAME _____ DATE _____

_____

_____

_____

LOVE FOR OTHERS

18

Though I speak with the tongues of men and of angels, but have not love,

I have become sounding brass or a clanging cymbal. . . . And now abide

faith, hope, love, these three; but the greatest of these is love.

1 Corinthians 13:1, 13

PRAYER

Lord, we all think we know something about love, and yet we have so much to learn. Love has so many facets. I pray for my child to experience all the facets of love, but especially Your love, the gift that convinces my child that You love him or her beyond measure, without condition. And in knowing Your love, give my child the capacity to love others.

"In this is love, not that we loved God, but that He loved us and sent His Son to be the propitiation for our sins. Beloved, if God so loved us, we also ought to love one another. . . . There is no fear in love; but perfect love casts out fear, because fear involves torment. But he who fears has not been made perfect in love. We love Him because He first loved us. If someone says, 'I love God,' and hates his brother, he is a liar; for he who does not love his brother whom he has seen, how can he love God whom he has not seen? And this commandment we have from Him: that he who loves God must love his brother also" (1 John 4:10-11, 18-21).

Some friends of ours made errors in business judgments, fell on hard times, and in the process lost their home and jobs. The wife's proud father was embarrassed by the situation and said to his daughter, "The best thing I could have done when you were a child was to pour fuel over you and torch you." Words like these—especially in a difficult time—are devastating. Words can kill just as surely as guns do.

Our words to our children are powerful, and even more powerful is the intent behind the words. If we give our children words of praise and encouragement, allowing for and forgiving their mistakes, they will respond positively. If we condemn our children by using language that puts them down or attacks their character, they will respond negatively to others and develop not only low self-esteem but also a false idea about who God really is.

The family setting is truly a crucible. The first step to making our homes safe, loving places is to recognize how quickly our homes can become unloving and harmful. In our weaknesses and selfishness, we all have the ability to hurt one another. And the deepest wounds can come from those who love us most.

We do enormous things to make love happen. We marry the right person and look for meaningful work. We try to get our biblical doctrines straight. We go to seminars and read books. And in the midst of this, we are assaulted by "unlove." Media blitzes come at us with new tales every day of molestation, abuse, exploitation, violence, and perversions of love until we cover our ears with our hands and cry, "Stop! I can't take any more of this ugliness!" And then sometimes, we see the unlove in ourselves.

Love cannot be forced. It is like the blossoming of a beautiful rose. God plants the seeds of love, then encourages, "Learn of Me." It is in

Love for Others

the learning, in the being drawn to him that it happens. Jesus says, "You can love, because I first loved you." To experience that love is a lifetime quest. Jesus tells us in a myriad of ways, "You are worth everything to me. I died for you." And yet often we hold Him at arm's length, accepting only teaspoonfuls of his love. Then we wonder why we can give away only teaspoonfuls of love to others.

In learning to accept God's love, we must realize that He has paid the full debt of our unlove. If we accept God's love for us and live in that love, we will love others.

What does love look like? It is difficult to describe. Love is part of empathy and understanding for our son. Love is part of covering a hard truth with a blanket of mercy. Love is part of a gentle touch for my spouse. Love is part of a simple, profound prayer from our daughter. Love is part of respecting ourselves as people with limits and failings, as people who need to be restored. Sometimes love hurts. Sometimes love must wait, giving freely without expecting response. And as the One who loves us most lifts the heavy yoke of sin and selfishness, we are able to love freely out of that fullness.

"Most of all, let love guide your life" (Col. 3:14, TLB).

I pray that my children will make it a lifetime quest to be people who love. Love is not the easy way. Love can be painful. Yet it is the fullest, richest way. It is the way of our Lord and reflects Him as nothing else does.

R E F L E C T I O N

"Most of us have just enough religion to make us hate,
but not enough to make us love."

Jonathan Swift

"The way of love is never an easy way. If our hearts be set on walking in that way,
we must be prepared to suffer. It was the way the Master went;
should not the servant tread it still?"

Amy Carmichael, *IF*

"The greatest thing . . . a man can do for his heavenly
Father is to be kind to some of His other children."

Henry Drummond, *The Greatest Thing in All the World*

F A M I L Y   I N T E R A C T I O N

1 Read this poem to your child, and discuss how love "includes":

> *"He drew a circle that shut me out:*
> *Heretic, rebel, a thing to flout.*
> *But love and I had the wit to win;*
> *We drew a circle that took him in."*
>
> —Edwin Markham

2 For a one-month period, use love as the theme of your family devotions. Read 1 Corinthians 13, small portions at a time. Ask each family member how he or she is doing in the ability to love.

C O M M U N I C A T I N G   T H E   B L E S S I N G

I pray for you, my child, to develop a deep love for others. I pray that as you accept God's love for you, you will be able to love not just the lovable people but also the unlovable ones. I pray that God will develop in you a love that weeps with the world and touches the forgotten and lonely people. As you give your love to others, may they see God's love for them.

MY PRAYER FOR MY CHILD

NAME _____ DATE _____

_____

_____

FOLLOW-UP PRAYERS, ANSWERS, AND INSIGHTS

NAME _____ DATE _____

_____

_____

Love for Others

LORD, HELP MY CHILD TO DEVELOP . . .

OPTIMISM

19

[Love] bears all things, believes all things, hopes all things, endures all things.

1 Corinthians 13:7

PRAYER

Lord, I pray that my child will see the positive side of life. Let my child have that rare ability to look for the best, even in the dark times. Help my child be a person who sees opportunities in problems. Help my child bring sunshine where there is rain, courage where there is fear, and hope when there is despair.

SCRIPTURE

"Finally, brethren, whatever things are true, whatever things are noble, whatever things are just, whatever things are pure, whatever things are lovely, whatever things are of good report, if there is any virtue and if there is anything praiseworthy—meditate on these things" (Phil. 4:8).

77

Our Andy has always had a lot of enthusiasm. He always has a contagious smile on his face and sees the best in people. His first week of first grade was exciting for him as he met a lot of people and thought they were all great. On Friday of the first week, he burst in the door from school. "Mom!" he shouted. "Guess what. Today I found out the school principal is a Christian!"

"Why, that's nice, Andy," I said. "How do you know?"

"Well, when all of us got on the school bus to come home, I heard Mr. Armbruster say, *'Thank God!'*"

It is always refreshing to be around people who are positive, who can look at a glass and see it as half-full, not half-empty. Colossians 3:1–2 says, "If then you were raised with Christ, seek those things which are above, where Christ is, sitting at the right hand of God. Set your mind on things above, not on things on the earth." True to our fallen natures, we need a conscious act of our will to set our minds on things above. For some of us, it is more of a discipline than for others. Bad news on television is popular because bad news has a ready audience. Gossip (sometimes disguised as a prayer request) spreads quickly because we find it so easy to think the negative.

In the magazine-publishing field, we would at times get a dozen positive letters on an article to one negative letter. Which letter do you think we noticed? The negative one! To look for the best in a situation is to take a trusting stance toward God, to make a faith statement. It says, "I know there's a possibility here."

Howard Lindsay once said, "Experience in business teaches that people are far more likely to agree with the optimist than to disagree. Conversely, people are far more likely to offer a no to the sour, gloomy pessimist. A pessimistic man's words may be completely unheeded or inspire a lack of confidence, but a healthy, vital, optimistic man uttering the same words may rock the world." We must remember that optimism is the first cousin to faith, and pessimism is the first cousin to doubt.

When I (Bill) was a boy, I went around after Christmas when people discarded their old Christmas trees. I collected a motley bunch of used trees and set up my own Christmas tree lot. Now *that's* optimism! That little spark of seeing the potential, of looking for the best, may have come through for me when we mortgaged our home to buy *Virtue* magazine, a fledgling magazine that was badly in debt. I read the readers' letters and realized that the magazine had good potential. Seeing the possibility was a faith statement. We bought the magazine, and *Virtue* has gone on to flourish and grow.

It is refreshing to be with people who are positive, who are thinking the best of us. We want to be with people like that because it is encouraging to us. Henrietta Mears, a Sunday school teacher who encouraged in their youth such influential leaders as Bill and Yvonne Bright, said, "It's not so much who you believe in, as who believes in you!" A person with optimism, with faith in the God of the impossible is a person who can influence his or her world.

I pray that my children will develop optimism toward life. I pray that they will have an unshakable confidence in Christ and believe that all things will work out for the good.

REFLECTION

"God has somehow placed into the Christian's insides a special something, that extra inner reservoir of power that is more than a match for the stuff life throws at us. When in operation, phenomenal accomplishments are achieved, some things even miraculous."

Charles Swindoll, *Come before Winter*

"You don't raise heroes, you raise sons. And if you treat them like sons, they'll turn out to be heroes, even if it's just in your own eyes."

Walter M. Schirra, Sr.

"As you travel through life, my brother, to have happiness untold, keep your eye upon the doughnut, and not upon the hole."

Anonymous

FAMILY INTERACTION

1 Ask your child to list five things that he or she does well.

2 Ask your child, "How do these things make you and other people happy?"

Optimism

3 It's easier for some to be optimistic than others, due to the difference in personalities. Read Philippians 4:6-9 as a family, and discuss each of your individual life approaches. Do you see life as a glass that is half-full or half-empty?

4 Put a jar with a "happy face" on a shelf. Every time someone in the family catches another family member being pessimistic, the pessimistic person must put a nickel in the jar. When the jar is full—we hope that doesn't happen too soon—give the money to a good cause.

COMMUNICATING THE BLESSING

I pray for you, my child, to develop optimism. You will make mistakes, have discouragements, and sometimes experience failure. That is part of being human. But never stop looking for the best in people, in yourself, in circumstances, and in what God can do.

MY PRAYER FOR MY CHILD

NAME _____ DATE _____

_____

_____

_____

_____

FOLLOW-UP PRAYERS, ANSWERS, AND INSIGHTS

NAME _____ DATE _____

_____

_____

_____

_____

LORD, HELP MY CHILD TO DEVELOP A . . .

PASSION FOR GOD

20

When You said, "Seek My face," my heart said to You, "Your face, Lord, I will seek."

Psalm 27:8

PRAYER

Lord, many people seem to be going through the motions of living. Work, leisure, and even worship seem to have little intensity or focus. I pray that my child will have a spiritual hunger and passion that will cause him or her to desire Your truth and righteousness. And in the pursuit of Your truth, may my child know that only You can answer that hunger.

SCRIPTURE

"Blessed are those who hunger and thirst for righteousness, for they shall be filled" (Matt. 5:6).

Our son Jon is famous in our family for his passion for learning. He has a quick, inquisitive mind, and nothing excites him as much as learning something new. His brothers tease him mercilessly at times about being "the professor." However, Jon is a very contagious person to be around because he is interested in so many things. It's wonderful to watch his passion for learning in the spiritual realm, too, as he pursues God's Word and good books with the same keen interest.

One of the best things about being around young people is their enthusiasm for life. Ecclesiastes 11:9 says, "Young man, it's wonderful to be young! Enjoy every minute of it! Do all you want to; take in everything, but realize that you must account to God for everything you do" (TLB). If we take care to awaken it, we will find a natural wonder of learning, a passion for God in our children.

My (Nancie's) mother had an irrepressible passion for life. I remember tromping across a dry Montana prairie with her when I was small. It was autumn, and we were collecting weeds for arrangements. We may as well have been walking in some famous, cultured garden for all the delight my mother saw in discovering beauty. Her delight was conta-

gious, though, and suddenly I saw beauty everywhere in the dry and dusty landscape. Her passion for learning and life and God led her into Bible studies, and through the years she became a much loved teacher. People came to hear her because she glowed with the love of what she was teaching. My own love for the things of God was fed by her passion for God.

Passion for the things of God is not something we often seek out or desire. We don't want to be too radical, too much of a fanatic, yet we want to pursue a passion for God. To live life with passion for God is to live it with love, with caring. Jesus had strong words for the church at Ephesus: "I have this against you, that you have left your first love" (Rev. 2:4). How is it that our passion for Christ, for living our very lives, gets quenched, smothered?

Knowing God—realizing the vastness of who He is and exploring His ways that are past finding out—is worth the pursuit of a lifetime. The more *interested* we become in the things of God, the more we become contagious.

Bill and I think back to when we were first in love; we both felt that no one else in the

Passion for God

world was as important to us as we were to each other. Amazingly, after twenty-eight years, that is still true! But back then, when love was new, we spent quality time together, showed each other our best side, took time to be considerate. It's too easy, now, to take each other for granted. If we are too busy, our love can be trampled, quenched. Things get boring. But passion can become renewed with time and care. Passion is one of God's great gifts that lets us know we're alive. Passion is being in touch with the full range of emotions that God has given to us.

Our life in Christ can become rote, boring, and predictable. We take Him for granted and go through the motions of living, not understanding that He is a real Person who longs for relationship with us. He is the one who brings healing, joy, and purpose to our lives. He intimately cares for us and longs for our response.

Some things in life are worth our passion: our relationship with Christ, our loved ones, our friends, and our calling. May we express that passion in whatever way God has gifted us creatively.

I pray that my children would live lives rich in passion for God. I pray that they would love Him, their "first love," with an all-consuming love that will not dim with the years. May that passion develop into beautiful maturity.

R E F L E C T I O N

"Set our hearts on fire with love to you, O Christ our God, that in its flame we may love You with all our heart, with all our mind, with all our soul, and with all our strength and our neighbors as ourselves, so that, keeping Your commandments, we may glorify You, the giver of all good gifts."

Eastern Orthodox Church

"Until religion becomes a passion, it is only a habit."

Anonymous

"If you have Shakespeare in you, what poetry you could write. If you have Beethoven in you, what music you could compose. But if you have Christ in you, what a life you can live!"

Anonymous

FAMILY INTERACTION

1 Ask your child, "What do you *love* to do? What makes you feel fully alive? What do you think it means to live life with passion?"

2 Discuss with your child this quotation by Arthur Rubenstein: "I have found that if you love life, life will love you back." What do you think this means?

3 Think of a passionate person your child will know. Talk with your child about that person's passion, affirming that quality and its expression.

COMMUNICATING THE BLESSING

I pray for you, my child, to develop a deep passion—for God, for life, for people. I pray that you will realize that the greatest quest in life is to know God, in the power of His resurrection and in the fellowship of His sufferings. I pray that when you express your passion, other people will see the depth of your love and want what you have—and want the Lord whom you love.

Passion for God

MY PRAYER FOR MY CHILD

NAME _____ DATE _____

_____

_____

_____

FOLLOW-UP PRAYER, ANSWERS, AND INSIGHTS

NAME _____ DATE _____

_____

_____

_____

LORD, HELP MY CHILD TO DEVELOP . . .

PURITY

21

Blessed are the pure in heart, for they shall see God.

Matthew 5:8

P R A Y E R

Lord, the word *virgin* seems almost foreign today. To many people, "having values" no longer means choosing God's purity, abstaining from sex outside of marriage, and fleeing temptation. Instead, values today are relative; people are encouraged to do as they please. Lord, help my child to be wise enough to choose the way of purity, to resist the sensual temptations that are so prevalent in this society. Teach us what it means to love You with an undivided heart, with all our heart, soul, mind, and body.

S C R I P T U R E

"Don't let anyone look down on you because you are young, but set an example for the believers in speech, in life, in love, in faith and in purity" (1 Tim. 4:12, NIV).

Our society, in its desperate pursuit of sexual freedom, is losing something very basic and precious. We as a culture have never been so educated and public about sex, and yet we have never been in such great sexual conflict. When pleasure becomes the driving force for everything we do, it is destructive to us and to those we love. Maggie Gallagher in *Enemies of Eros* writes, "Men and women come to feel we have a right—a *natural* right—to sex without pregnancy. We feel our bodies are betraying us when sex leads to babies. Unless, of course, the pregnancy is chosen, then it is the rational act of the mind, rather than the mere, despised, mindless mechanisms of the body, which is the true author of the miracle of birth."

The sexual part of our being is very powerful; it is at the core of who we are. It is the God-given force that forges marriages, produces children, nourishes families. When we do not respect our bodies and when we ignore the boundaries and experience sexual intimacy outside of marriage, it causes deep repercussions. A friend told me (Nancie), "I wish someone had told me a long time ago that when God made me, He included instructions. These instructions define His love for me and His wish that I avoid things that will numb, hamper, or destroy me. Sexual purity is not a law; it's a sacred recipe for life. It

brings freedom. When you don't use the recipe, you face sexually transmitted disease, abortion, single parenthood, delayed dreams, broken promises, and even death. A lot is at stake! What *isn't* at stake is God's love for us. Kids today need to understand the connection between spirituality and sexuality, because it's this connection that will give them the power to be pure. I wish when I had asked the question, someone would have told me something about myself rather than giving me a rule I didn't understand."

The church at Corinth struggled with sexual immorality. The apostle Paul instructed them: "Flee sexual immorality. . . . He who commits sexual immorality sins against his own body. Or do you not know that your body is the temple of the Holy Spirit who is in you . . . and you are not your own? For you were bought at a price; therefore glorify God in your body and in your spirit, which are God's" (1 Cor. 6:18-20).

To glorify God in our bodies is a lifelong stance. God has given us this gift of sexuality as a vital part of our being, and its full expression is found in the sanctity of the marriage relationship. We can reinforce in several ways this concept to our children when they're hearing conflicting messages from our culture.

First, we can honor our marriage commitments as a model to our children. Our children need to see the joy and fulfillment that a lifelong commitment can bring. Young love with its excitement can fade as the years go by, and the "spark" can get quenched. Making our sexual relationship a priority is a key to keeping a marriage alive. Several times Bill and I have gone away for time "just for us." We tell our children, "This is an investment in your lives as well."

Second, we must talk to our children about the value of sexual purity. The word *purity* can carry negative connotations—that of restriction, of prudishness, of condemnation. Nothing could be further from the truth. In *How and When to Tell Your Kids about Sex,* Stanton and Brenna Jones emphasize the importance of teaching our children about the beauty and blessedness of sexual intercourse within marriage—a "life-uniting" process. When people practice sexual intercourse outside of marriage, it is as if they have received a priceless painting as a gift but have chosen to use it as a TV tray on which to serve and spill popcorn and soft drinks.

Third, it's never too late to start talking with our children about purity. It's better to start talking about sexual purity when our children are young, but if you haven't already started, start today. Remember the principle of God's forgiveness—none of us is beyond redemption. God gives us laws and principles because He loves us infinitely.

I pray that my children will realize the importance of sexual purity, that they will save the gift of sexuality for the person whom God has selected for them to marry. May God help us as parents to convey the beauty and sanctity of what it means to remain sexually pure.

R E F L E C T I O N

"Our Lord often calls His church His bride. Like a bride of beauty and purity in no other color than white, all Christians represent that they are pure, 'spiritual' virgins awaiting the joys and intimacies of heavenly marriage with their Groom."

Charles Swindoll, *Growing Deep in the Christian Life*

"A pornographic culture is not one in which pornographic materials are published and distributed. A pornographic culture is one which accepts the ideas about sex on which pornography are based."

Maggie Gallagher, *Enemies of Eros*

FAMILY INTERACTION

1 If your children are adolescents, no doubt they have heard about condoms or other forms of birth control. Discuss the ramifications of what it means to have authority figures endorse birth control for teenagers.

2 Prayerfully plan a special time when you and your pre-teen can talk about sex and sexuality. Excellent materials are available, such as James Dobson's *Preparing for Adolescence,* Richard and Renee Durfield's *Raising Them Chaste: A Practical Strategy for Helping Your Teen Wait Till Marriage,* and Stanton and Brenna Jones's *How and When to Tell Your Kids about Sex.*

3 Let your child know you are praying for his or her future spouse (if they express a desire to be married someday), the "special one" God has somewhere for him or her.

COMMUNICATING THE BLESSING

I pray for you, my child, that you develop purity. Your mind and body are wonderful gifts the Creator has given to you. Be a good steward of all He has given you, and I pray that you can resist temptations that would derail you from wholeheartedly being His.

MY PRAYER FOR MY CHILD

NAME _____ DATE _____

_____

_____

FOLLOW-UP PRAYERS, ANSWERS, AND INSIGHTS

NAME _____ DATE _____

_____

_____

LORD, HELP MY CHILD TO DEVELOP A SENSE OF . . .

$\mathcal{F}$AIRNESS

22

And what does the Lord require of you? To act justly and to love mercy

and to walk humbly with your God.

Micah 6:8, NIV

PRAYER

Lord, I pray that my child will be free from racism, bigotry, and bias. Help my child to play by the rules and in accordance with the law, having respect for everyone, regardless of differences. Give my child a clean heart and a clear conscience, untarnished by the world. When my child is tempted to take advantage of a situation, remind him or her that the weak and disadvantaged ones are special in Your eyes.

"Open your mouth for the speechless, in the cause of all who are appointed to die. Open your mouth, judge righteously, and plead the cause of the poor and needy" (Prov. 31:8-9).

I N S I G H T

One of the earliest things a child learns is what is fair and what is not. Lots of things in life are not fair. One of the things we've noticed about the middle child in our family is that he has a well-developed sense of what is fair. Sandwiched between the two oldest and the two youngest, he has a good perspective. When he was eight years old, he wrote us a note: "Dear Mom and Dad. Thank you for treating me fair and that you do not favor. I know you know that's wrong. Love, Chris." We laughed but realized he was just keeping us on our toes, reminding us to be just in our dealings.

The mother of King Lemuel agonizes over what to tell her son: "What, son of my vows? . . . Open your mouth for the speechless, in the cause of all who are appointed to die. Open your mouth, judge righteously, and plead the cause of the poor and needy" (Prov. 31:2, 8-9). I (Nancie) join that mother. I want our children to speak out on the injustices in our society, especially for the powerless, who cannot speak out. The injustices in the world can be overwhelming. While we obviously can't right all the wrongs, we can help the powerless people around us.

We parents must be fair with our children. When we demonstrate a sense of fairness to our children, we encourage them to be fair with their peers. We also need to be careful not to allow bigotry and bias to take root in families. We need to be careful that our economic position in life does not lull us into accepting the status quo. What would have happened if courageous people like Harriet Beecher Stowe, John Brown, and Abraham Lincoln had not taken a stand for abolishing slavery?

The key to being fair is found in the New Testament: "Let nothing be done through selfish ambition or conceit, but in lowliness of mind let each esteem others better than himself. Let each of you look out not only for his own interests, but also for the interests of others" (Phil. 2:3-4).

I pray that my children will be fair in their dealings, giving credit to whom it belongs, considering other people's lives and well-being. I pray that they will move beyond looking out only for their own needs. And in doing so, may they fulfill the law of love.

"How does one determine whether a law is just or unjust? A just law is a man-made code that squares with the moral law or the law of God. An unjust law is a code that is out of harmony with the moral law. To put it in the terms of St. Thomas Aquinas: an unjust law is a human law that is not rooted in eternal law and natural law. Any law that uplifts human personality is just. Any law that degrades human personality is unjust. . . . Was not

. . . Jesus an extremist for love: 'Love your enemies, bless them that curse you'?

. . . Amos an extremist for justice: 'Let justice roll down like waters and righteousness like an ever-flowing stream'?

. . . Paul an extremist for the Christian gospel: 'I bear in my body the marks of the Lord Jesus'?

. . . Martin Luther an extremist: 'Here I stand; I cannot do otherwise, so help me God'?

. . . John Bunyan: 'I will stay in jail to the end of my days before I make a butchery of my conscience'?

. . . Abraham Lincoln: 'This nation cannot survive half slave and half free'?

. . . Thomas Jefferson: 'We hold these truths to be self-evident, that all men are created equal'?"

Martin Luther King, Jr., letter from Birmingham city jail

Fairness

"We need fairness whenever we share our selves with each other. Fairness is at stake in every conversation, in every sharing of duties, in every argument, in every syllable of the communications of love. . . . Fairness needs love as the seed in the cold earth needs the nurture of the warming sun. But love needs fairness as the flowing river needs its firm clay banks. Love may be the heavenly vision, but fairness is the guiding light."

Lewis B. Smedes, *A Pretty Good Person*

F A M I L Y   I N T E R A C T I O N

1 Say to your child, "Tell me about a time when you felt you were treated unfairly." Listen. Ask, "How did it feel to be treated unfairly? Why is it important that we try to be fair?"

2 Let your child know that life isn't always fair: Some kids are born into poor families; some have handicaps; some are born addicted to drugs. Talk about how each of you can go out of your way to try to be fair to those who do not have the advantages you have.

3 Talk about judges and the court system. Discuss how the job of judges is to try to be *fair* to all people.

C O M M U N I C A T I N G   T H E   B L E S S I N G

I pray for you, my child, to develop a sense of fairness. Keep in mind that taking advantage of others grieves God, but fairness pleases Him.

MY PRAYER FOR MY CHILD

NAME _____ DATE _____

_____

_____

_____

_____

_____

FOLLOW-UP PRAYERS, ANSWERS, AND INSIGHTS

NAME _____ DATE _____

_____

_____

_____

_____

LORD, HELP MY CHILD TO DEVELOP A SPIRIT OF . . .

GENEROSITY

23

Give, and it will be given to you. A good measure, pressed down,

shaken together and running over, will be poured into your lap.

For with the measure you use, it will be measured to you.

—*Luke 6:38, NIV*

PRAYER

Lord, help my child to be a giver rather than a taker. Help my child to experience the joy of giving. May my child be swift to give time, talent, money, possessions, thanks, compliments, healing words, smiles, love, hugs, and a hand or an ear, whenever the opportunity presents itself.

"Cast your bread upon the waters, for you will find it after many days. . . . He who observes the wind will not sow, and he who regards the clouds will not reap. . . . In the morning sow your seed, and in the evening do not withhold your hand; for you do not know which will prosper, either this or that, or whether both alike will be good" (Eccles. 11:1, 4, 6).

I N S I G H T

Some people just know how to give; other people have to work at it. Our friend Cindy always seems to know how to give just the right gift, card, or some personal touch that makes us feel loved.

Generosity does not just mean sharing personal possessions or giving of things, although that is part of it. True generosity comes from a full heart. Stingy people can't give because they feel they have nothing to give. They are trying to protect what little they have, not realizing it will get smaller and smaller. The wonderful thing about generosity is that it ends up blessing the giver. Proverbs says, "A generous man will prosper; he who refreshes others will himself be refreshed" (Prov. 11:25, NIV).

Holidays, birthdays, and special events are good opportunities for children to learn to give as well as to receive. When Jon and Eric were nine and seven, Bill had to be gone over Mother's Day. Before he left, he talked with the boys and gave them some money

with the instruction to "get something really special for Mom for Mother's Day."

The Saturday before Mother's Day, the boys asked if I (Nancie) would drive them to Kmart. I stayed in one part of the store with the two younger boys while they did their shopping. Soon they came up to the front of the store where I was waiting, smiles on their faces and a box in their hands—a box *with breathing holes in it.* Yep, that was the Mother's Day I got two hamsters: Simon and Garfunkel. Every mother should be so lucky. I had a sneaking hunch that this "gift" wasn't really meant for me.

It is a beautiful thing to give out of the heart, with no strings attached, to give something that is the very essence of our being. I loved getting gifts from our children when they were small because the gifts were so authentically an expression of each child. When Chris was eight, he spent a lot of time making a Mother's Day card for me, decorating it with flowers. On the outside of the card he wrote, "Happy Mother's

Generosity

Day," and on the inside he wrote, "I'll never forget you." (I'll bet he won't!)

Then there was the Christmas that Eric did his Christmas shopping for the whole family in ten minutes. He was in a candy store, and he thought, *Why not?* So he got nine little bags of chocolate (fifty-cents worth each), taped them shut, wrote whom they were for on the out-side of the bags, and tossed them under the tree. The problem was that during the several days left before Christmas, he couldn't resist poking holes in the bags and taking a bite or two. Eric's intentions were good—he was just giving with a few strings attached.

The truth is that giving is a joyful experience. A person with a generous spirit has so much more joy than someone who isn't generous. The paradoxes of the gospel of Christ are true here as well: Give, and you receive.

I pray that my children will develop a spirit of gen-erosity, that they will give out of a full heart even out of an empty heart if need be. Help me be a parent who demonstrates generous giving to my children.

R E F L E C T I O N

"Generosity is not merely a trait which pleases God. It is a practice which releases us from bondage to self, and also to things."

Albert E. Day, *Discipline and Discovery*

"Not what we give, but what we share, For the gift without the giver is bare; Who gives himself with his alms feeds three, Himself, his hungering neighbor, and me."

James Russell Lowell

"Generosity is like a rare gem. Not many of us possess it, but when it is seen, it sparkles. What admiration it brings from onlookers. Are you sparkling today? Or have you misplaced the gem called generosity?"

Charles Swindoll, *Growing Strong in the Seasons of Life*

F A M I L Y   I N T E R A C T I O N

1 Find a person or family in need in your community (people who are sick, housebound, in a rest home, homeless, etc.). Take your child with you as you take the person some food, money, blankets, clothing, books, or flowers. Discuss the experience.

2 Consider doing an ongoing family project that would help someone who is in need. This could involve helping an elderly neighbor with errands or yard work. Discuss with your family how you can give to a certain person or family on a consistent basis, making a real investment in their lives. Doing these giving projects is truly putting legs to prayers. These types of projects will cost you time, but the rewards are great!

3 Ask your child, "How do you feel when you give generously to other people?"

C O M M U N I C A T I N G   T H E   B L E S S I N G

I pray for you, my child, to develop a spirit of generosity. I pray that you will learn that it really is more blessed to give than to receive. I pray that you will know the joy in having a generous spirit, that you will be a wise and faithful steward of all that you have been given.

MY PRAYER FOR MY CHILD

NAME _____ DATE _____

_____

_____

FOLLOW-UP PRAYERS, ANSWERS, AND INSIGHTS

NAME _____ DATE _____

_____

_____

LORD, HELP MY CHILD TO DEVELOP . . .

TRUST

24

Trust in the Lord, and do good; dwell in the land, and feed on His faithfulness.

Psalm 37:3

PRAYER

Lord, You are so trustworthy, yet I often find myself doubting Your Word, fearful of life, questioning the way I take. It is so easy to want to steer our own ship through the storms of life. Help my child to trust in Your Word and in Your way. Give my child that divine confidence that comes from following You both into the wilderness and onto the mountaintop. And help my child to be trustful and trustworthy with associates and friends.

SCRIPTURE

"Trust in the Lord with all your heart, and lean not on your own understanding" (Prov. 3:5).

We live in the forest of the Cascade mountain range in central Oregon, and we see deer who visit our backyard daily. As I (Bill) write this, I count fifteen does and fawns ambling through the trees, nibbling the manzanita brush. Our neighbors on both sides of us have put out salt licks, another added attraction. We have also discovered that the deer love oats. Now when Nancie goes to the store, Amy often asks her to get an extra box of oats for the deer.

One day this fall, Amy went out to the back-yard to leave some oats for the deer who were meandering through the trees close to our deck. When they saw her with the box of oats, they came closer. She held out a handful of oats and stood motionless. Closer they came, to about ten feet away. She could almost see their agony, wanting to munch the oats but fearing to come any closer. Their noses sniffed toward Amy while their big brown eyes looked as if they were saying, "Can I trust you not to harm me if I come closer?"

Finally one young doe, as if to defy natural instinct and suppress that fear, took a few more steps toward Amy, stretched out her neck and began to nibble the oats from Amy's hand. Amy grinned as the other deer stood watching as if in amazement. Since that time, this one doe has become Amy's friend.

She eats oats from Amy's hand regularly— even to the point where she will nuzzle Amy's shirt, begging for more when the oats have run out. But the other deer still will not eat from Amy's hand. Their instinct of fear and mistrust continues to prevent them from taking those last few steps toward "oat bliss."

Too often, that is the way I am with God. I don't want to abandon my preconceived notions. God beckons me to run toward Him in complete trust, but I hold back, not want-ing to give up control. My human tendency is to want to reach out to grasp God with one hand while clinging to what I think I know with the other . . . just to be safe.

Mercifully, our God is a longsuffering, good God. He holds His goodness out to us, His children, and we move toward Him to eat our fill. In feeding on His Word, in practical experience, we learn that He is to be trusted.

Nancie's grandmother was widowed during the Great Depression, left to raise four small children. With no Social Security, it was a hand-to-mouth existence. As the years went by, she made a commitment to follow Christ. It was not an overnight victorious walk but a gradual, deepening trust that God would pro-vide for her. Nancie's earliest memories of

Grandma Olson—when she was not a whirl-wind of activity helping on the farm—are of watching her sit in her rocking chair, reading her Bible. She drank in the words as if they were her very life. And they were. The words of her favorite hymn were, "Jesus, Jesus, how I trust Him, how I've proved Him o'er and o'er. Jesus, Jesus, precious Jesus. O for grace to trust Him more."

We are not in a Great Depression; we don't worry about our next meal. And yet in these stress-filled, fearful times, we have many opportunities to choose trust over fear. I wonder what our children's impressions will be of our trust in God. Psalm 71:5 says, "For You are my hope, O Lord God; You are my trust from my youth."

I pray we will have grace to trust Him more and more, abandoning ourselves to His goodness.

I pray that my children will learn to trust God and not be afraid. I pray that at the times when they are fearful or worried, they will choose to trust. I pray that the Scriptures will become living nourishment for them, showing strength, purity, and redemption.

R E F L E C T I O N

"I am to trust in my Lord without hesitation and without reservation— with all my heart—so that He might step in and take control, making my way meaningful and straight."

Charles Swindoll, *Stress Fractures*

"That the Almighty does make use of human agencies and directly intervenes in human affairs is one of the plainest statements in the Bible. I have had so many evidences of His direction, so many instances when I have been controlled by some other power than my own will, that I cannot doubt that this power comes from above."

Abraham Lincoln

F A M I L Y   I N T E R A C T I O N

1 Blindfold one member of the family and lead him or her to an undisclosed destination. After you get there, take off the blindfold. Ask, "How does it feel to be led, not knowing where

you're going?" Did the family member trust you? Why or why not? Take turns doing this, and then discuss how it feels to trust.

2 Read Psalm 37 together. Discuss what is difficult about trusting God and what is wonderful about it. What are ways, as an individual and as a family, to grow in trust?

3 Talk with your child about some experiences that helped you learn to trust. Don't be afraid to be vulnerable. Looking back, how did these trying experiences prepare you to trust God in the future?

COMMUNICATING THE BLESSING

I pray for you, my child, to develop trust. I pray that you will learn to trust God no matter what happens. I pray that you will prove yourself trustworthy to others. I pray that you will learn to trust the people who love you.

MY PRAYER FOR MY CHILD

NAME _____ DATE _____

_____

_____

_____

FOLLOW-UP PRAYERS, ANSWERS, AND INSIGHTS

NAME _____ DATE _____

_____

_____

_____

LORD, BLESS MY CHILD WITH . . .

Assurance

Comfort

Creativity

Dreams

Good Friends

Health

Joy

Laughter

A Love of Learning

Mentors

Music

Opportunity

Originality

Peace

Safety

PART 3

LORD, BLESS MY CHILD WITH . . .

*A*SSURANCE

25

Let us draw near [to God] with a true heart in full assurance of faith . . .

for He who promised is faithful.

Hebrews 10:22-23

P R A Y E R

Lord, many people think that Your love is conditional, Your grace limited, Your forgiveness temporary. Sometimes I feel that way myself because of my own limited capacity for love, grace, and forgiveness. I pray that my child, after making a personal confession of faith, will grow to be absolutely certain of what he or she knows. Guard my tongue and my attitude from implying otherwise.

S C R I P T U R E

"For I know whom I have believed and am persuaded that He is able to keep what I have committed to Him until that Day" (2 Tim. 1:12).

Last week we were driving our thirteen-year-old daughter, Amy, home from church camp. She told us about her experience of committing her life to Christ. "But I want to know something," she said earnestly. "How do I know God is there? I pray to Him, but I can't see Him."

Bill responded, "Do you remember when Mom and I were gone to Russia for eighteen days?"

She did, all too well. It had been difficult for us to be away from our children that long. Since we had been in a remote part of Russia, we hadn't been able to phone home. So we contented ourselves with letters and pictures, waiting for the day when we would be reunited.

"Jesus was here on earth," we reminded her, "and went back to heaven. We read the Bible, His 'letters' to us, and wait for the day when we will be together with Him." We also talked about the wind: We can't see the wind, yet we feel its effects and know it's there. And we can't see love, yet we know love is real.

If we are honest, we will admit that all of us at times have Amy's questions. "Is God there?" "Does He really care about me?" "How do I know I belong to Him?" "How can we *know*?"

When I (Nancie) was a teenager, the world was opening up to me in wonderful yet stunning ways. I began to be aware of the evils in the world: the war in Vietnam, the horrors of the Holocaust, racial injustice. I wondered, *How can a God of love and justice allow these things to be?* I carried these tortured wonderings inside for many months. Then one night while I was doing dishes with my mother, I blurted out, "Mother, I don't believe there is a God!"

She listened to me for a while and laughed a little as she said, "Of course God is there. But it's OK that you're asking questions. He is there. He'll always be there for you."

Her reaction disarmed me, and I wondered later, *What made her so sure?*

My mother's words were true: God has been there for both of us when we have had times of testing and difficulty. Now I realize my mother was so sure because God had proved Himself to her. As she took steps of faith to trust Him, He was there for her.

God is bigger than our doubts, our fears, and our humanity. He can handle our questioning.

My (Bill's) mother, who grew up in an alcoholic home, came to know God through a

Assurance

neighbor. She now looks back at that time when she accepted Christ and says, "I threw myself wholly on Him, and my sole strength became God."

God is not only our parents' God, He is *our* God—He is *my* God. Now we long for our children to know God for themselves, to know that He is intimately involved in their lives, to know He loves them. We long for God to become our *children's* God.

Often our prayers for our children center on keeping them safe, shielding them from harm, from the evil one. And yet we can't alter the fact that they must come to God on their own. We know that coming to know God personally is often the result of personal crisis, an awareness of our own inadequacy, haunting questions, up-against-the-wall times.

While we know that suffering can strengthen us, we find it hard to see our children struggle. We don't want our children to suffer, and yet if we are praying for God's highest purpose in their lives, we must continually yield our children to God, pray with thanksgiving, and look to the big picture in their lives.

What do we pray for our children? We pray that they will know God, that they will have an assurance that He is *their* God. We pray that our children will learn what it means to trust God in both the good and the bad times. We pray that our children can take that step of faith and believe God, trusting that He is there and that His Word is true. He is the all-perfect Father God, and He can be trusted.

I pray that my children will "know whom they believe," that they will become persuaded through faith in God alone, that He is their God, their Lord, their protector.

R E F L E C T I O N

"Only one Person can step into a life and give it happiness even when health fails and give it peace even when possessions fade and give it security even when savings fly away."

Charles Swindoll, *Growing Strong in the Seasons of Life*

"I was going around in a circle until Jesus gave me a compass."

Lynn Langley

FAMILY INTERACTION

1 Tell a story about a time when you lacked assurance, had doubts, or felt insecure. Ask your child if he or she has ever felt that way.

2 Look up some Scripture verses that assure us that God loves us no matter what (John 3:16; Rom. 8:38-39; 1 John 3:19-20; 1 John 4:12-18). Talk with your kids about God's unconditional, no-matter-what love for us.

3 Talk about the whys of life. Why do people suffer (starvation, natural calamities, cancer, death at a young age)? We don't always know how to answer the whys, but we do know that God asks us—even children—to trust Him. When we can't see the answers with our eyes we must trust God's character.

COMMUNICATING THE BLESSING

I pray for you, my child, that you would know assurance. God's love is not like our human love. We often put conditions on love, but God loves without measure. God's love is for eternity. He keeps on loving you no matter what. Remember, there is no pit so deep that God can't swoop down and rescue you.

MY PRAYER FOR MY CHILD

NAME _____ DATE _____

_____

_____

FOLLOW-UP PRAYERS, ANSWERS, AND INSIGHTS

NAME _____ DATE _____

_____

_____

LORD, BLESS MY CHILD WITH . . .

Comfort

26

In the multitude of my anxieties within me, Your comforts delight my soul.

P s a l m   9 4 : 1 9

PRAYER

Lord, You know how I struggle with anxiety. When I look at the world my child must live in, I see so much potential for problems. But then You pour in Your comfort, saying, "I am here. Don't be afraid." Father, today I pray for my child to be blessed with comfort, Your warm assurance that You are with us in the midst of life and that everything's all right.

SCRIPTURE

"I, even I, am He who comforts you. . . . And I have put My words in your mouth; I have covered you with the shadow of My hand" (Isa. 51:12, 16).

It is a difficult thing to watch our children suffer loss, and yet that is part of the parenting experience. Losses come in many shapes and sizes and are painful to mourn. Our son Chris had a dog bite that injured his lip. It was a loss, in a sense, because he was unable to play his trumpet for a while. He was in junior high at the time, and his trumpet playing had given him a sense of self-worth and confidence.

We remember watching our son Eric during his senior year in high school sob after a final, crucial basketball game as he saw his dreams for competing at the state finals evaporate.

Comfort

Amy, our daughter adopted from Korea, went through a time of deep pain and anger at the enormous loss of her identity, her language, her birth parents—a loss so huge it was hard to comprehend. One night, after an emotionally stormy day, she confessed, "I feel so lost. I feel as if my whole world is upside down." When Nancie's mother died recently, Amy sobbed, "I don't want to lose her." None of us did, and we cried as we held each other.

It is satisfying to be able to comfort our children in the midst of their troubles, even when we can do nothing to restore the loss. When our children allow us to comfort and cradle them emotionally, we feel a deep sense of wholeness. It feels as if this is one of the moments for which we have been created. In the midst of comforting our children, both of us experience healing, warmth, bonding, and restoration.

The losses children experience are very real. We must not trivialize our children's feelings, because those painful experiences can stay with them for a lifetime. How healing it is to have a parent understand and express love during a time of loss. The Scripture says when we "bear one another's burdens" we "fulfill the law of Christ" (Gal. 6:2).

Jesus has given us the model. When we feel loss in our lives, Jesus—our parent, our High Priest—comforts us. He knows what we are feeling. He is touched by "the feeling of our infirmities" (Heb. 4:15, KJV).

A groomsman at the recent wedding of our son Jon was a childhood friend who was going through a wrenching divorce. In the midst of Jon's happiness, the wedding brought to Jon's friend a fresh reminder of the loss of his own marriage. I noticed the young man's parents hug their son immediately after the wedding and ask how he was doing. It was beautiful to watch as they offered comfort and hope to their son, in essence saying, "You are not alone. We know how you feel, and we love you." As these parents reached out in understanding and compassion, they demonstrated to their son the love and comfort of God.

Jesus said, "Let not your heart be troubled." What is most comforting is simply the presence of the Lord, who loves us, brings us in, washes us, cleanses us, and holds us in His arms. When we identify with our children and respect their feelings, we demonstrate God's character to them. Our very presence with them through tough times gives our children comfort.

I pray that in my children's inevitable losses, they will turn to the "God of all comfort." May I be God's arms of comfort in my children's lives. Help me bear their burdens and comfort them by being there for them.

R E F L E C T I O N

"God, it has been said, does not comfort us to make us comfortable, but to make us comforters. Lighthouses are built by ex-drowning sailors. Roads are widened by mangled motorists. Where nobody suffers, nobody cares."

W. T. Purkiser

"God's hand is in your heartache. Yes, it is! If you weren't important, do you think He would take this long and work this hard on your life?"

Charles Swindoll, *Encourage Me*

F A M I L Y   I N T E R A C T I O N

1 Ask your child to tell you about a time or place in which he or she felt safe. Ask the child to explain why he or she felt safe. Discuss the fact that all of us need to feel that safe place at times.

2 Discuss with your child a time when a pet or a friend was sick or injured. Talk about how the child wanted to comfort the pet or friend. Let your child know that God wants to do that for us when we hurt.

3 Ask your child, "Where would you go if you felt you were in trouble or in danger?" Then remind your child that God is always there to help, comfort, forgive, and heal.

COMMUNICATING THE BLESSING

I pray for you, my child, that you would know comfort. In the losses of your life, may you experience the sweet presence of the Holy Spirit. Remember that the Bible tells us, "Blessed are those who mourn, for they shall be comforted."

MY PRAYER FOR MY CHILD

NAME _____ DATE _____

_____

_____

_____

_____

_____

Comfort

FOLLOW-UP PRAYERS, ANSWERS, AND INSIGHTS

NAME _____ DATE _____

_____

_____

_____

_____

_____

LORD, BLESS MY CHILD WITH . . .

CREATIVITY

27

For since the beginning of the world men have not heard nor perceived by the ear,

nor has the eye seen any God besides You, who acts for the one who waits for Him.

Isaiah 64:4

P R A Y E R

You, Lord, are the great Creator. You created us in Your image, giving us the wonderful ability to be creative. Lord, help my child not just to watch others create via television, movies, art, literature, and music but to be one who expresses You through his or her gifts. Give our family the discipline to turn off the television and do something together to bring a sense of Your beauty to our lives.

S C R I P T U R E

"You are worthy, O Lord, to receive glory and honor and power; for You created all things, and by Your will they exist and were created" (Rev. 4:11).

111

During the Civil War, George Washington Carver was born to a slave woman owned by Moses Carver. George spent lots of time outdoors, helping on the plantation. Here his gifts took shape. He loved every flower and plant. He practiced sketching plants with amazing accuracy and beauty. Young Carver would talk to God as he looked at various plants—the peanut, the sweet potato—asking the Creator to show him the secrets hidden in each plant. Years later, Carver became a world-renowned botanist, head of agricultural research at the Tuskegee Institute in Tuskegee, Alabama. One of Carver's favorite sayings was, "You're well equipped for what you choose: you have arms and legs and a brain to use."

Inherent in all of creation is the reflection of God's indescribable creativity. Not all of our children will be famous botanists, artists, or musicians, but because they are God's creations, our children possess His creative character. Inside each human being is a force that delights in creativity.

Children are naturally creative. Each of them has a different way of expressing that creativity. We have enjoyed watching how our five children have expressed their individual creativity. Our oldest son, Jon, has always loved music. We can see it gives him pleasure to express himself through music. Eric, our second oldest, is gifted athletically. He can see instinctively how to plan a game, what offenses to run, what strategies to employ. Chris, our middle son, is a writer. Nothing makes him happier than holing up in his room with a computer and pounding out a story or creating a poem. Andy is gifted at making people smile. His banter and humor can make people feel good. He also knows how to use his humor in his writing. Amy, our youngest, gets much satisfaction out of drawing and sketching. She also expresses her creativity through origami, folding paper to make animals and birds.

As parents, we can provide the environment to foster creativity: reading to our children when they're very small, encouraging dialogue and imagination. We can expose them to all styles of music and to opportunities to take music lessons. We can encourage them to use the library. We can turn the television off, making sure we provide lots of good books, drawing materials, paints, clay, and other raw materials for them to use.

After we do these things, we can observe our children. What seems to make them come alive? In what areas do they express confidence? In what areas do we see special strengths? As we see our child excel in or enjoy a certain creative expression, we can affirm that expression. As we look back at the extraordinary life and giftedness of George Washington Carver, we see that Moses Carver, the owner of the plantation on which young Carver was raised, encouraged the boy in his love for nature, discovery, drawing, music, and reading. Strengthened by that affirmation, George Washington Carver explored his many gifts with awe and wonder, realizing that they were an expression of his Creator's character.

Creativity is simply expressing the unique person that God has made each of us to be.

Expressing our creativity brings joy and satisfaction, and it allows other people to catch a glimpse of God's character. Expressing our creativity is a way of cooperating with our Creator in being the kind of person He has made us to be.

I pray that my children will find their unique area of expressing creativity. May they use their giftedness to give back to the Lord, the ultimate Creator. I pray that their creativity will give joy to others and that through their giving they may experience personal satisfaction in creating something good, wholesome, and beautiful. Use me as their parent to help them unlock the creativity placed inside them.

REFLECTION

"You take the pen, and the lines dance.
You take the flute, and the notes shimmer.
You take the brush, and the colors sing.
So that all things have meaning and beauty in that
Space beyond time where you are.
Now then, can I hold back anything from You?"

Dag Hammarskjöld, *"God the Artist"*

"Creativity is so delicate a flower that praise tends to make it bloom, while discouragement often nips it in the bud. Any of us will put out more and better ideas if our efforts are truly appreciated."

Alexander Osborn

1 Sit outside with your child and look at the stars. Later, read Psalm 8 and discuss the majesty and the wonder of creation.

2 Ask your child, "How do you feel when you look at this awesome display of God's creativity?"

3 Ask your child, "What do you like to make? What expression of creativity gives you pleasure or makes you feel complete inside?"

4 Read Psalm 139 with your child, reminding your child of how precious he or she is to our Creator. After all, we are His creations, the work of His hand.

COMMUNICATING THE BLESSING

I pray for you, my child, that you will find full expression in creativity. One of the greatest joys you will ever have is to express the creativity that God has placed inside you. To create something that is beautiful and that reveals who you are is to reflect God's character. Don't be satisfied with being passively entertained. Instead, cultivate the joy of giving of yourself in creating for others.

MY PRAYER FOR MY CHILD

NAME _____ DATE _____

_____

_____

FOLLOW-UP PRAYERS, ANSWERS, AND INSIGHTS

NAME _____ DATE _____

_____

_____

LORD, BLESS MY CHILD WITH . . .

DREAMS

28

Where there is no vision, the people perish.

Proverbs 29:18, KJV

PRAYER

O God, in this world where visions are brutally treated, where Your law is destroyed, and where dreams are crushed, I pray that my child's dreams will be protected. Keep Your holy Word written on my child's heart, on tablets of flesh, that Your Word will take root in his or her life, giving hope and dreams for the future.

SCRIPTURE

"When the Lord brought back the captivity of Zion, we were like those who dream. Then our mouth was filled with laughter, and our tongue with singing. Then they said among the nations, 'The Lord has done great things for them'" (Ps. 126:1-2).

In a tall ponderosa pine close to our house hang the tattered remnants of a kite. One spring break fourteen years ago, our son Jon went out to fly a kite. It danced too close to the trees, and it got stuck there. When we had bought that kite, the salesperson in the kite shop told us that the kite had a lifetime guarantee. If we could return even a small piece of the kite, we could get it replaced. So we tried shooting arrows, throwing rocks—everything—to get a piece of the kite, stuck forty feet up in the tree. Recently, after a wind storm, we found a worn piece of the kite on the ground. Unfortunately, the kite shop where we bought the kite has gone out of business. Not even kite shops have lifetime guarantees!

When we were first married and lived in San Francisco, we had no money, but we were rich with dreams. We used to go down by the marina and fly kites. Somehow the experience was symbolic of our dreams—watching a lovely thing take off in the wind, letting it sail.

As parents, we can keep our children's dreams alive by affirming their interests and their gifts. We can *look* at their painting, *listen* to their musical piece, *read* what they have written, *cheer* at their basketball games.

Observe your child. Identify areas in which he or she shines. Then encourage him or her in those areas. Help your child see the finer, more beautiful aspects of his or her goals.

We can nourish our children's dreams when we tell family stories of faith or accomplishment through adversity. Our stories and encouragement help them see that dreams are the first step to possibilities. We can read good books to them of adventurers, of explorers, of heroes of the faith. In this culture, we must work at restoring the possibilities of dreams for our children.

Two months ago, Jon married Brittni, a beautiful young woman with dreams of her own. At their rehearsal dinner, we gave them a gift—a kite. "Take this on your honeymoon," we suggested, "and fly it together. Dream some big dreams for God. When your kite gets stuck in a tree, you can dream a new dream. And remember that some things *do* have a lifetime guarantee:

- God will never leave you or give up on you.
- His Word is true, and He encourages us to keep dreaming, to sail in the wind of His Spirit.
- We, your parents, will love you always."

I pray that my children will keep their precious dreams, that the enemy would not crush them. I pray that they will persist in dreaming about the wonderful, helpful, beautiful things possible for them to do and be. I pray that they will have vision and that their lives will be vibrant.

R E F L E C T I O N

"A crucial part of real-world faith building . . . is to connect one's life to an overarching dream or a consuming idea. . . . For centuries, people have speculated about the key change that Jesus instigated in the lives of His followers when He came to this world. I believe the key change was the dream He gave them—the dream of the kingdom of God."

Gordon MacDonald, *Christ Followers in the Real World*

"Give the dreamers room. Go easy on the 'shouldn'ts' and the 'can'ts,' OK? Dreams are fragile things that have a hard time emerging in a cloud of negativism— reminders like 'no money' and 'too many problems.'"

Charles Swindoll, *The Quest for Character*

"Cherish your visions; cherish your ideals; cherish the music that stirs in your heart, the beauty that forms in your mind, the loveliness that drapes your purest thoughts, for out of them will grow all delightful conditions. . . . 'Ask and you shall receive.' Dream lofty dreams, and as you dream, so shall you become. . . . The greatest achievement was at first and for a time a dream. The oak sleeps in the acorn; the bird waits in the egg; and in the highest vision of the soul a waking angel stirs. Dreams are the seedlings of realities."

James Allen, *As a Man Thinketh*

"God never gave us a dream without the strength to carry it out."

Anonymous

FAMILY INTERACTION

1 Ask your child, "What do you dream of doing or becoming?"

2 Ask your child, "Have you had a dream come true? Is there a dream that you think is too impossible for you? What is the dream, and why do you think it is impossible?"

3 Say to your child, "Describe the kind of person you think God wants you to become. In what ways can you start fulfilling these goals?"

4 Read Romans 12 together, and discuss what gifts God has given each of you. Discuss how you are using your gifts. What talent or gift might you have buried or left unused? How might each of you become better stewards of God's gifts?

COMMUNICATING THE BLESSING

I pray for you, my child, that you will hang on to your dreams. Sometimes those dreams will be changed or reshaped. But as you hang on to your faith in God, you will realize that, indeed, all things are possible through Him. Sail in the wind of His Spirit.

MY PRAYER FOR MY CHILD

NAME _____ DATE _____

_____

_____

_____

FOLLOW-UP PRAYERS, ANSWERS, AND INSIGHTS

NAME _____ DATE _____

_____

_____

LORD, BLESS MY CHILD WITH . . .

GOOD FRIENDS

29

A man who has friends must himself be friendly,

but there is a friend who sticks closer than a brother.

Proverbs 18:24

PRAYER

Lord, I pray that You will give my child that special person—in addition to family members—who will always love, accept, believe in, and defend him or her. Let it be the kind of friendship that allows my child to have a safe place for confidence and trust. I pray that this friend will be a godly person who encourages my child toward better things, toward a closer relationship with You.

"Greater love has no one than this, than to lay down one's life for his friends. . . . No longer do I call you servants . . . but I have called you friends" (John 15:13, 15).

Winnie the Pooh and Piglet—the best of friends—were walking down the road together. Piglet slipped his hoof into Pooh's paw. "Yes, Piglet?" said Pooh.

"Nothing," said Piglet. "I just wanted to be sure of you."

The best thing about good friends is that they *are there*. Good friends know us so well that we don't have to explain much to each other. Robert Louis Stevenson wrote, "A friend is a present you give yourself." But tending a friendship and keeping lifelong friends takes effort. You don't have intimate friends unless you invest something of yourself in the relationship, develop a history together, weather good times and bad times together. Proverbs 17:17 says, "A friend loves at all times, and a brother is born for adversity."

Friendships take work. We call our friends, spend time together, remember them on birthdays or other special days, even when we move miles apart. Our children get the idea

of how important friends are by the priority we parents place on our own friendships and by the way we talk about our friends in front of our children.

Do we welcome our children's friends into our homes? Our attitude toward our children's friends is reflective of our attitude toward our children. They take it personally. When Eric was three, we moved to another city and left behind the only house and neighborhood he had known. To protect himself, he made up an imaginary friend that he called Charlie Beakey. Charlie was an integral part of our family life for about a year.

Amy has a dear friend named Wendy. Wendy is a youth pastor's wife and the mother of two small children, but somehow she finds the time to write to Amy, remember her on her birthday, and call occasionally. Her letters mean a great deal to Amy, and Amy keeps a picture of Wendy's family on her bulletin board. We are grateful to Wendy, as she is a good role model for Amy.

Good Friends

What a wonderful strength friends can be, especially good friends. A dear friend gave us a card that read, "Friendship is the relationship we all need to help us through our other relationships." Friends can also be detrimental, which is why we pray for *good* friends for our children. An old proverb says, "Keep company with good men and good men you will imitate." Especially in the pre-teen, teen, and young adult years, friends seem to have more influence than parents do. That is why it is so important for us to give our children safe places to make quality friendships: the life of the church, sports programs, part-time jobs, etc. Active, thriving friendships based on activities and faith are a healthy foundation for friendships to grow. While we can't pick our children's friends, we can help lay the groundwork where good friendships will flourish.

I pray that my children will have good friends, that they will develop the skills to make lasting friendships, and that they will choose their friends wisely. May their friends bring joy and comfort to them as well as a greater awareness of the best friend anyone can have—Jesus.

R E F L E C T I O N

"If we advance through life and do not make friends, we shall soon find ourselves alone. We must keep our friendships in constant repair."

Samuel Johnson

"A man must not choose his neighbor: he must take the neighbor God sends him. . . . The neighbor is just the one who is next to you at the moment, the one with whom any business has brought you into contact."

C. S. Lewis

"We cannot tell the precise moment when friendship is formed. As in filling a vessel drop by drop, there is at last a drop which makes it run over; so in a series of kindnesses there is at last one which makes the heart run over."

James Boswell

1 Ask your child to name someone who has really listened to him or her.

2 Discuss how your child feels to be around that person.

3 If your child has lost good friends, talk about why that happened and what can be done to avoid it. Share stories of how you lost friends too. Discuss with your child how he or she can be a good friend.

4 It seems harder for some people to make friends than others. Ask each other:
- How am I doing at being a friend?
- Am I making new friends, taking care of old friends?
- What does it take to be a friend?

COMMUNICATING THE BLESSING

I pray for you, my child, that you will have good friends. You'll discover this to be one of the most precious treasures in life. I pray that you will tend these relationships with time and commitment. Not everyone has good friends, but everyone needs them. Those who are blessed with even one good friend are rich beyond measure.

MY PRAYER FOR MY CHILD

NAME _____ DATE _____

_____

_____

FOLLOW-UP PRAYERS, ANSWERS, AND INSIGHTS

NAME _____ DATE _____

_____

_____

LORD, BLESS MY CHILD WITH . . .

HEALTH

30

Beloved, I pray that you may prosper in all things and be in health,

just as your soul prospers.

3 John 1:2

PRAYER

Lord, I pray for my child to be healthy. You have given this child into our care, and I want him or her to experience spiritual, physical, and mental health. We know that is what You want for us too as Your children. Teach my child how to become balanced in life, to take time for rest, to find satisfying work, to look for mental stimulation, to take care of the temple of Your Spirit, the body.

SCRIPTURE

"My son, give attention to my words. . . . Keep them in the midst of your heart; for they are life to those who find them, and health to all their flesh" (Prov. 4:20-22).

Without question, we parents want our children to be healthy. Right from the very first hours of our children's lives, it is the usual pattern to have a pediatrician examine them, making sure they are healthy. We get them started as tiny babies on immunizations. We make sure they have vitamins and fluoride for strong teeth. We check their growth, carefully monitoring their development. We try to see that they eat a well-balanced diet.

Some of our most distressing moments have been when our children were sick. We have sat by our children's sides as they have had surgeries: Andy had surgery to repair an eardrum; Chris once had surgery to put tubes in his ears and another time had surgery to repair scar tissue from a dog bite on his lip. Eric and Chris were both hospitalized at times with pneumonia. Jon once had a rare anaphylactic reaction that was difficult to diagnose and treat.

Parents never outgrow this concern for their children's well-being. One of the last things my (Nancie's) mother said to me before she died was that I should get more sleep. Bill's parents call frequently to ask how we're doing. They want to know if we are healthy. We also check on our grown-up kids, asking if they're eating right, if their allergies are active.

"How are you?" we ask one another, sometimes as a habit, but often as a gauge, a measuring stick of how another is feeling.

As parents with a godly perspective, we want our children to be healthy spiritually and mentally too. We want their souls to prosper as well as their bodies. A balanced approach toward life involves honoring God with our whole beings, worshiping God with our whole selves. Romans 12:1-2 articulates this plea from Paul: "I beseech you therefore, brethren, by the mercies of God, that you present your bodies a living sacrifice, holy, acceptable to God, which is your reasonable service. And do not be conformed to this world, but be transformed by the renewing of your mind, that you may prove what is that good and acceptable and perfect will of God."

We can promote physical health by watching our diet and exercising regularly. But we must have a broader definition of health. More and more evidence suggests that most illnesses and diseases are caused by stress. A few years ago I (Nancie) was having severe health problems. I went to one of the country's best clinics for a thorough evaluation. The diagnosis? Stress. I realized I was not living a balanced life—mentally, physically, and spiritually. I had neglected my body and was not resting as I should. I needed to lighten up, to remember that I was human, not superwoman. I had to take time for beauty and fun. I have learned valuable lessons about respecting this temple that God has given me.

These days as we are being educated more about how to care for our environment and about what it takes to be good stewards of this world that God has given us, it's good to remember that each of us is a uniquely created temple of God. We are given the responsibility to be stewards of our own bodies and minds. We each have individual weaknesses and strengths, with individual vulnerabilities. One of our sons tends to let pressure get to him; another of our sons never seems to have a problem with it.

We all need to remember that our bodies are "the temple of the Holy Spirit who is in you. . . . Therefore glorify God in your body and in your spirit, which are God's" (1 Cor. 6:19-20).

I pray that my children will experience health, a balanced approach to life that gives them a base for a good, successful life. I pray that they will have health of body, spirit, soul, and mind.

R E F L E C T I O N

"The four main requirements of good mental health as outlined by a staff member of an internationally known psychiatric hospital are
1. A variety of sources of satisfaction in daily life.
2. Ability to demonstrate a flexibility under stress.
3. Understanding and acceptance of one's own strengths and weaknesses.
4. Understanding of others as individuals."

Kentucky School Journal

"A man too busy to take care of his health is like a mechanic too busy to take care of his tools."

Spanish proverb

"Your body is far more intricate than the federal highway system. Inside you are some 100,000 miles of nerve fibers along which messages zip at speeds of 300 miles per hour."

Hal Boyle

Health

F A M I L Y   I N T E R A C T I O N

1 Ask your child what he or she is learning in school about good health.

2 Suggest that each family member keep a log for a week on how well he or she takes care of himself or herself. Make a chart, and at the end of each day, list food eaten, exercise, fun activities, reading, time with friends, work, sleep, etc. At the end of the week, assess how each of you has done, noting the areas to improve.

3 Discuss our need to have healthy minds. Ask your children how this can happen. "What we feed our minds dictates what our minds will become." Healthy minds feed on wholesome thoughts and ideas, just as healthy bodies feed on wholesome food.

C O M M U N I C A T I N G   T H E   B L E S S I N G

I pray for you, my child, that you will be blessed with health, that you will take responsibility for honoring the temple of the Holy Spirit that is you. I pray that you will do things that are good for you, knowing that this is an important way to express love for yourself, God's creation.

MY PRAYER FOR MY CHILD

NAME _____ DATE _____

_____

_____

_____

FOLLOW-UP PRAYERS, ANSWERS, AND INSIGHTS

NAME _____ DATE _____

_____

_____

Health

LORD, BLESS MY CHILD WITH . . .

JOY

31

These things I have spoken to you, that My joy may remain in you,

and that your joy may be full.

John 15:11

PRAYER

Lord, You never promised that we would be perpetually happy, but You do promise joy. Help my child to be filled with joy, that inner peaceful confidence and assurance that You are there and that Your love is constant, regardless of circumstances.

SCRIPTURE

"Looking unto Jesus, the author and finisher of our faith, who for the joy that was set before Him endured the cross, despising the shame, and has sat down at the right hand of the throne of God" (Heb. 12:2).

Joy

One day when Chris was a high school senior, he was reading through our old high school yearbooks. He was amused to see glimpses of his parents as young people: a college boy known for his pranks and a carefree schoolgirl. Chris flopped back on the couch with a disgruntled look. "What is it, Chris?" I'd asked.

He said grimly, "I just realized these are my 'good old days,' and I'm not having any fun!"

Joy is not fun, and it's not happiness, even though joy and happiness are good things. Happiness is dependent on outside stimulus: the right circumstances, how I am treated, whether or not I am enjoying health and prosperity.

It's difficult to teach our children the difference between joy and happiness because their whole world seems to be wonderful or awful, depending on how their hair turns out in the morning or on the grade they got in math class. Bill always makes a point of telling Amy how great she looks before she leaves for school and that he loves her. Even though that may seem like insignificant background noise to her now (what's *really* important is her hair), this is a basis for joy in her life—the secure knowledge that no matter how bad things get, she is loved. *Joy is claiming that knowledge.*

Joy has a deep quality, and we see from Scripture that joy comes out of obedience, out of endurance. In the Book of Nehemiah is the story of how Jerusalem was rebuilt after being destroyed and laid waste for many years. Nehemiah, who was devastated at the ruins, was given permission by the king to go back and rebuild the city. He enlisted the help of others who used to live in the city. The expert masons and carpenters went to work. Even though the workers were attacked by enemies, they worked with a weapon in one hand and a tool in the other. Through amazing teamwork, the wall around the city was built sooner than the people had expected. Then the workers began to restore the buildings within the walls. When the workers finished their project, the priests called the people together and read the Scripture to them. The people wept as they listened. Then they entered into a feast and celebrated, sharing what they had with others. Nehemiah told them, "The joy of the Lord is your strength" (Neh. 8:10).

We parents are no different from our children. We can have the notion that when our circumstances are all going well, *then* we will have that elusive quality of joy. But joy often comes unexpectedly—maybe after times of endurance, of rebuilding. We realize that

God's presence is there, and joy overflows. We realize that he has been there all the time, loving us as a Father.

When we look back to our own childhoods, we remember experiencing joy, often when we were with our families: Bill on hunting trips with his dad, Nancie outside on her family's farm, savoring the beauty of the outdoors. But what brought joy was the deep, underlying knowledge of being loved and free to enjoy life.

Not long after Chris was worried about not having any "fun," he and his mom went on a spur-of-the moment hike to the top of some bluffs. Nancie will never forget the breathtaking moment of reaching the top to see what lay beyond: a meadow that stretched far below, a river winding through it, against the backdrop of the pristine snow-covered Three Sisters Mountains. That was a moment of joy, taking in the beauty with her son, even though along with the joy, she felt pain in knowing Chris would soon be leaving home. Joy comes from knowing the security of our Father's love and care through all the changes of life. We are reminded in 1 Timothy 6:17 to "trust in . . . the living God, who gives us richly all things to enjoy."

I pray that my children would have deep, abiding joy in their lives, the joy that comes from obedience, from walking with Jesus in the good times and the challenging times.

R E F L E C T I O N

"As the hand is made for holding and the eye for seeing,
You have fashioned me for joy.
Share with me the vision that shall find it everywhere;
in the wild violet's beauty; in the lark's melody;
in the face of a steadfast man; in a child's smile;
in a mother's love; in the purity of Jesus."

Gaelic prayer

"One joy scatters a hundred griefs."

Chinese proverb

"A joy shared is a joy doubled."

Johann Wolfgang von Goethe

FAMILY INTERACTION

1 Read together Psalms 86, 103, and 104. Using these passages, discuss what God is like. How can knowing this give us joy?

2 A phrase in 1 Thessalonians 2:19-20 talks about people being our joy. How can a person be someone's joy?

3 Is your child a joy to you? Tell your child what makes him or her a joy.

4 Talk about the difference between joy and happiness. (Happiness is pleasant circumstances. Joy is inner peace, confidence, and assurance in spite of our circumstances.)

COMMUNICATING THE BLESSING

I pray for you, my child, that you will be blessed with joy. I pray that you will treasure joy over happiness. Joy is a by-product that happens—wonderfully, surprisingly—as you obey Christ. I pray that you will discover joy to be one of God's greatest gifts.

MY PRAYER FOR MY CHILD

NAME _____ DATE _____

_____

_____

_____

FOLLOW-UP PRAYERS, ANSWERS, AND INSIGHTS

NAME _____ DATE _____

_____

_____

_____

Joy

LORD, BLESS MY CHILD WITH...

LAUGHTER

32

He who is of a merry heart has a continual feast.

Proverbs 15:15

PRAYER

Lord, I think You enjoy seeing Your children laugh. I also want my children to have a good sense of humor, to enjoy a good belly laugh, to smile often, to recognize good comedy. Bless my children with fun times. Give them the ability to laugh at themselves and not take life too seriously.

SCRIPTURE

"He will yet fill your mouth with laughter and your lips with shouts of joy" (Job 8:21, NIV).

When our children were babies, Bill would say, "I *love* hearing them laugh!" Even now, when our children are older and are together playing board games or just being silly, it is so good to hear them laugh. Laughter is too often a casualty of an overstressed family. When laughter is thin around our house, it's a sign that we're pushing too hard and need to lighten up. Our Lord came to give us joy, not stress.

Some of our best family memories are the spontaneous moments. One day just before the school bus came by to bring the kids home, our dog, Chester (the ugliest dog you ever saw), was at my feet while I was folding laundry. Chester always went out to meet the kids. I had a pair of Andy's Superman Underoos in my hand and thought, *Why not?* So I put them on Chester and sent him out to meet the kids.

The gales of laughter from the boys at the sight of Chester were worth it.

Then there was the time when we had just come home from a speaking assignment in England. We had bought a tea set and were quite taken up with the English tea. Our yard was full of neighborhood boys, and we thought, *Why not have high tea with the neigh-*borhood boys? We put out the finest china and some dainty pastries and called in the kids. It was so funny to see them in their T-shirts and scruffy jeans, drinking tea, crooking their little fingers, trying to have manners.

We all laughed a lot. It feels so good to laugh.

Once while writing a book, I (Nancie) had to leave home for a few days because I needed to be away from interruptions. So I packed up my books and computer and drove to the coast for a few days. I got to my room and unpacked. Before I started to work, I climbed down the stairway to the beach. I stood at the railing, suddenly in awe of the beauty—seven miles of beach, waves rolling in, a lighthouse on a rocky cliff off in the distance. And I started to laugh. All by myself, I couldn't help it. It was just all too beautiful. And it occurred to me that laughter is really a form of praise—praise without words, but praise nevertheless. Laughter says, "God, thank you for creating me. Thank you that I'm alive. Thank you for this moment, these people, this place. I rejoice in You!"

And the Lord must surely delight in our laughter as we do in our children's.

I pray that my children will have laughter in their lives, that somehow they will be able to see humor in situations, even in difficult times. I pray that they will know the wonderful release of full-body laughter. I pray that they will discover the laughter that is praise to God.

R E F L E C T I O N

"God is a God of laughter, as well as of prayer . . . a God of singing, as well as of tears. God is at home in the play of His children. He loves to hear us laugh."

Peter Marshall

"I think it is often just as sacred to laugh as it is to pray, or preach, or witness."

Charles Swindoll, *Growing Strong in the Seasons of Life*

*"Not only in the words you say,
Not only in your deeds confessed,
But in the most unconscious way
Is Christ expressed.*

*"Is it a beautiful smile,
A holy light upon your brow?
Oh no! I felt His presence
When you laughed, just now.*

*"For me 'twas not the truth you taught
(To you so clear, to me so dim)
But when you came to me, you brought
A sense of Him.*

*"And from your eyes He beckons me,
And from your lips His love is shed
Till I lose sight of you, and see
The Christ instead."*

Anonymous, "Christ in You"

Laughter

F A M I L Y   I N T E R A C T I O N

1 Have a family member tell a favorite joke.

2 Recall a funny story of something you experienced as a family. Discuss how laughter can bring healing to tense situations. Discuss how laughter can hurt other people.

3 Read a funny book or watch a comedy together.

C O M M U N I C A T I N G   T H E   B L E S S I N G

I pray for you, my child, that you will be blessed by laughter. Learn to laugh with people, not at them. If you're going to poke fun, poke fun at yourself first. And remember, life is too important to be taken seriously.

MY PRAYER FOR MY CHILD

NAME _____ DATE _____

_____

_____

_____

_____

FOLLOW-UP PRAYERS, ANSWERS, AND INSIGHTS

NAME _____ DATE _____

_____

_____

_____

_____

Laughter

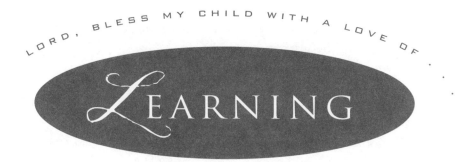

LORD, BLESS MY CHILD WITH A LOVE OF . . .

LEARNING

33

Be diligent to present yourself approved to God, a worker who

does not need to be ashamed, rightly dividing the word of truth.

2 Timothy 2:15

PRAYER

I pray that my child will have a love of learning. Let it begin with stories from the Bible and then overflow to classic stories of love, hope, and adventure. Help me to be faithful in reading to my child and in feeding my child's imagination and ability to understand. I pray that my child's quest for knowledge will continue through life. More than anything, I pray that my child will desire to know You more and more.

SCRIPTURE

"The fear of the Lord is the beginning of knowledge, but fools despise wisdom and instruction" (Prov. 1:7).

Children naturally want to learn. It's a necessary component to growth, like eating. Learning is a healthy part of maturation. Sometimes we see this appetite for learning stifled, and it's sad to watch the spark in a child's eye go out when learning stops being enjoyable.

Parents can help feed our children's natural desire to learn. Then other people—Sunday school teachers, schoolteachers, coaches, librarians—can further fan into flames our children's love of learning.

Not long ago we accompanied our daughter's class on a field trip to a fish hatchery. We watched as the forest ranger showed the critical importance of environment to the trout's healthy development. We watched him carefully adjust the water temperature and use long tweezers to remove some impurities from the tanks where the eggs grew.

The same dynamic applies to our homes as learning places. Environment is key to learning good, healthy things, and we parents have the privilege and responsibility to monitor what is there. We can't overestimate the importance this earliest development has on children. The formative years are precious and vital. We must watch the impurities that can filter in from the world, and make our homes wonderful places to develop.

Here are some practical helps to encourage love of learning:

- Read to your children even when they are infants.
- Ask your children questions about what you've read.
- Make sure that schoolwork and reading always come before television.
- Make a library just for your children's books.
- Stock your family bookshelves with quality books.
- Equip your children's study area with a dictionary and reference books.
- Visit libraries and museums often.
- Be involved with your children's school and teachers.
- At mealtimes talk about current events and what's going on in everyone's lives, making sure everyone gets to talk.

A love of learning makes for a long, productive life. On our local school board is an eighty-three-year-old board member, Clifton Clemens. We remember one school board meeting when Clifton gave a report of a recent trip he had made to the state legislature. He was curious, he said, how a bill was passed and made into law. He explained the whole procedure to the group, his eyes sparkling. "I never realized before this how laws were made, and it was so interesting." It was beautiful to see the animation in his character-lined face as he glowed with the love of learning something new.

The quest to know God, the secret places of His will, and the riches He has placed all around us is a lifelong adventure! Our own attitude toward God, toward learning new things about God and life is passed on to our children. Hosea 6:3 says, "Let us know, let us pursue the knowledge of the Lord.

Each new day, each new experience and challenge of life is an opportunity to learn something new about God.

I pray that my children will have a love of learning. I pray that this love will burn in them through their whole lives. I pray that at the base of my children's learning will be the desire to know God and the secrets He has stored for them in His world.

R E F L E C T I O N

"Grow dear friends; but grow, I beseech you, in God's way, which is the only effectual way. See to it that you are planted in grace, and then let [Him] . . . cultivate you in His own way."

Hannah W. Smith, *The Christian's Secret of a Happy Life*

"Listen, my son, to your father's instruction and do not forsake your mother's teaching."

Proverbs 1:8, NIV

"We cannot live our lives constantly looking back, listening back, lest we be turned to pillars of longing and regret, but to live without listening at all is to live deaf to the fullness of music. . . . But . . . what quickens my pulse now is the stretch ahead rather than the one behind, and it is mainly for some clue as to where I am going that I search through where I have been."

Frederick Buechner, *The Sacred Journey*

FAMILY INTERACTION

1 Ask your child, "If you could learn about anything in the whole wide world, what would it be?"

2 Ask your child, "What do you most like about learning?" Share with your child your answer to this question.

3 Ask your child, "What would learning about good things do for you? What would learning about evil things do for you?" Share your answers to these questions.

4 Ask your child, "What does it mean that 'The fear of the Lord is the beginning of knowledge'?" (Prov. 1:7).

COMMUNICATING THE BLESSING

I pray for you, my child, that you love to learn. What you feed your mind is what you are, so first of all, feed it with God's Word, the ultimate truth. I pray that you will feed your mind with good words and great works of gifted authors so that you will walk in wisdom in this world.

MY PRAYER FOR MY CHILD

NAME _____ DATE _____

_____

_____

_____

FOLLOW-UP PRAYERS, ANSWERS, AND INSIGHTS

NAME _____ DATE _____

_____

_____

LORD, BLESS MY CHILD WITH . . .

*M*ENTORS

34

Timothy, my dear son: . . . I constantly remember you in my prayers. . . . I remind you

to fan into flame the gift of God, which is in you through the laying on of my hands.

2 T i m o t h y   1 : 2 - 6 ,   N I V

P R A Y E R

Lord, I can only do so much to teach and be an example. My child will learn life principles from many other people besides me. Help my child find godly men and women who can be models and teachers. Give them moral coaches, inspired professors, ethical bosses, and anointed pastors.

S C R I P T U R E

"We were well pleased to impart to you not only the gospel of God, but also our own lives, because you had become dear to us" (1 Thess. 2:8).

Many years ago in a small Eastern European country, there lived a young girl named Agnes. In those early days before communism's grip on the country, her family was well-known in the community for its musical parties and for its piety. Little Agnes usually went with her mother as she tended the needs of the poor, bringing them relief and offering prayers for them.

The little girl that followed in her mother's shadow grew up to be the world-renowned Mother Teresa of the Sisters of Mercy of Calcutta, India. No doubt just being with her mother, who was intimately involved with ministry to the poor, had a profound influence on Agnes. That influence, in turn, has affected millions of people—the poor whom Mother Teresa and her co-workers serve as well as many people who have looked to Mother Teresa as a model.

All children need mentors. A child's first mentor is usually a parent. Then as children grow older, they look beyond the family to other people and voices to help them grow.

When our son Eric left for college a few years ago, he called and told us about a great law professor who taught at the school. He said, "Guess what, Dad! Mr.

Westbrook says that you spent time with him when he was a little kid. He told me after class that you had been important in his life then, and he wants me to have a weekly breakfast and Bible study with him and a few other guys." I (Bill) remember when I was Eric's age and was a youth pastor and grade-school teacher in a church in southern California. The pastor there had a young son named Ed. At the time I didn't think much of it, just that it was fun to spend some time with Ed. We often played catch in the park across the street from the church. Now twenty-eight years later, the tables were turned, and our son was being mentored—by the same person whom I had informally mentored when he was a boy! What a great feeling, especially since we were nine hundred miles away.

For three years, Ed faithfully had fellowship, Bible study, and prayer with Eric and other guys on campus. Eric has often told us that some of the most meaningful times of his college life were times spent with Ed.

Thedore G. Soares writes, "A young Harvard student . . . had read Charnwood's *Lincoln* and had been so impressed with the moral power of the hero that he had seemed to go through his daily life thinking as Lincoln thought and doing as Lincoln did. Then it occurred to him that that was what was meant by Christian living, so he read the story of Jesus in the Gospels and was again inspired with the ideal. He asked if he were right in thinking that he had come into religious experience. Of course he had come into the very heart of it, and was repeating the experience of Paul: 'For me to live is Christ.' Here were conduct models. . . . Great souls have more often liberated the souls of their disciples, enabling them to do and to dare in their day and for their generation as the great examples had done for theirs."

We all need mentors, someone who has walked the path ahead of us as we journey toward Christ.

I pray that my children will be blessed with mentors who will come into their lives and show them how to live the Christian life with integrity, honesty, and purpose. I pray that my children will recognize good, healthy mentors in their lives.

R E F L E C T I O N

"In the next year or so my signature will appear on $60 billion of United States currency. More important to me, however, is the signature that appears on my life— the strong, proud, assertive handwriting of a loving father and mother."

Katherine D. Ortega, former U.S. treasurer

"Someday, somewhere, I shall see what my life has come to mean to those who have watched me live."

Virgil Reed (Nancie's father), *Gift of Family*

"There is no influence so powerful as that of the mother."

Sarah Josepha Hall, American pioneer and writer

F A M I L Y   I N T E R A C T I O N

1 Ask your child, "What people have been good models to you? What was it about those people that made a difference in your life?" Share with your child the stories of several people who have been mentors in your life.

2 Ask your child, "If you could be like someone else, who would you want to be like? Why?" If your child names a person you feel would be a good mentor for your child, help him or her be able to have contact with that person. If the person is a character in a book or a historical figure, gather more information about the person for your child.

3 Ask your child, "What positive things in your life would make people want to follow you?"

COMMUNICATING THE BLESSING

I pray for you, my child, that you will be blessed with godly mentors, wise and righteous men and women who will challenge and inspire you for God's best in your life.

MY PRAYER FOR MY CHILD

NAME _____ DATE _____

_____

_____

_____

_____

FOLLOW-UP PRAYERS, ANSWERS, AND INSIGHTS

NAME _____ DATE _____

_____

_____

_____

_____

LORD, BLESS MY CHILD WITH . . .

*M*USIC

35

And the ransomed of the Lord shall return, and come to Zion with singing,

with everlasting joy on their heads. . . . sorrow and sighing shall flee away.

Isaiah 35:10

PRAYER

Lord, it's said that music is the language of the soul. It is part of Your creation. Yet some music is on the dark side and leads my child toward evil. Bring into my child's life music that lifts the soul and inspires goodness. Help my child reject music that destroys the soul.

SCRIPTURE

"My heart is steadfast, O God; I will sing and make music with all my soul" (Ps. 108:1, NIV).

It was after midnight, and our fifteen year old wasn't home yet. Andy and a buddy who was going to spend the night had gone to a football game with a friend who had just gotten his driver's license. This was a new experience, letting Andy ride with a driving friend. We stared at the clock and tried to be rational. Where could they be? They were already an hour late.

Then we heard it, way off in the distance. Our two dogs began to bay in response. *What's going on?* we wondered. It sounded like singing. We heard the back door open softly and the sound of muffled laughter. Andy poked his head into our bedroom. "Hey, Mom and Dad. How come you're not asleep?"

We sat up. "Where have you been?" Bill asked. "We've been worried sick!"

"Oh, I'm sorry. The gate across our road was locked, and we didn't have a key, so my friend dropped us off. We walked home—almost three miles. It was so dark we could hardly see anything but the stars, but it was *awesome!* We sang all the way home."

The boys went upstairs, and both of us had to laugh. Here they were, out celebrating their

youth, singing under God's beautiful stars, while we, the mature ones, huddled under the blankets and worried. (We asked Andy the next morning what they had sung. He said, "We sang 'Ninety-Nine Bottles of Beer on the Wall' until we got to our corner, then we started singing 'Amazing Grace'!")

What is it about music that transcends words? What is the spirit behind singing, especially a cappella singing? Music can be intimate communication with God. In church a hymn or praise chorus is not just notes and harmony. It means fellowship with others in our walk of faith, in our adventure with God. When we sing "Marvelous grace of our loving Lord, grace that exceeds our sin and our guilt," I (Nancie) see Grandmother Olson, an early widow who raised her four children through the Great Depression. That song was the theme of her life.

"Great Is Thy Faithfulness" reminds us of our parents: They came to know the Lord when they were young, struggling to earn livings, raise families—all in utter dependence on God. At times when the world is "too present" and when I have no words to express my feelings, I find myself humming a song to God: "I just want to be where You are, dwelling in Your presence." God inhabits the

M u s i c

praises of His people, and He is near to us when we sing to Him (Ps. 22:3).

We had a Thanksgiving celebration this year with our daughter-in-law's family. The Esteps are very warm and loving people, and it was a special time of blending two families together. Brittni's mother said, "We can't wait until you sing!" Our son had told them our tradition of singing a hymn before we sat down. We had not consciously drilled the idea of singing into our children; it has just been something we've done because we grew up with it and find it a wonderful means of expression.

Using music is a lasting way to get God's Word and a sense of worship into our children's lives. We can use the old hymns as well as the contemporary praise songs and choruses that incorporate Scripture. Play them in your home or in your car. You may be surprised at how meaningful this can be in your children's lives.

I pray that my children's lives will be blessed with music, beautiful music. I pray that music will flood their lives, lift up their souls, and help them worship our great Redeemer. I pray that they will find full expression in this wonderful gift of music.

R E F L E C T I O N

"A little boy who loved music was bitterly disappointed because he could neither play nor sing. But Amati, the violin maker, said: 'There are many ways of making music. What matters is the song in the heart.' So Antonio Stradivarius was encouraged to become the world's greatest violin maker."

Edgar Chrisemer

"There must be always remaining in every man's life some place for the singing of angels, some place for that which in itself is breathlessly beautiful and, by an inherent prerogative, throws all the rest of life into a new and creative relatedness, something that gathers up in itself all the freshest of experience from drab and commonplace areas of living and glows in one bright white light of penetrating beauty and meaning—then passes. Despite all the crassness of life, the hardness of life, the harsh discords of life— life is saved by the singing of angels."

Howard Thurman, *Deep Is the Hunger*

FAMILY INTERACTION

1 When your child chooses to play quality music or sing a wholesome song, affirm him or her. When you hear your child listening to music on the radio, tape deck, or CD player, ask him or her what is appealing about the music. Listen to your child's response and affirm what you can.

2 Ask each family member to talk about his or her favorite hymn and what special meaning the hymn has. Read Ephesians 5:19: "Speaking to one another in psalms and hymns and spiritual songs, singing and making melody in your heart to the Lord."

3 Sing together as a family. Find a hymnal and incorporate singing in your worship. Sing to Him anywhere—driving in the car, working around the house.

COMMUNICATING THE BLESSING

I pray for you, my child, that God will bless you with a love for music. I pray that music will bring out what's best and noblest in you: the love of life and beauty, creativity and harmony, the desire to dance for joy, an array of healthy emotions, and a desire to worship God.

Music

MY PRAYER FOR MY CHILD

NAME _____ DATE _____

_____

_____

_____

FOLLOW-UP PRAYERS, ANSWERS, AND INSIGHTS

NAME _____ DATE _____

_____

_____

146

LORD, BLESS MY CHILD WITH . . .

OPPORTUNITY

36

Look carefully then how you walk . . . making the most of the time.

Ephesians 5:15-16, RSV

PRAYER

Lord, bless my child with opportunities to speak Your name, to testify to Your goodness, to influence others for righteousness. I also ask that You bless my child with opportunities to love and be loved, to experience the joy of close friendship, and to have fulfilling employment. Give my child power to resist opportunities to cheat, lie, or take advantage of others.

SCRIPTURE

"Therefore, as we have opportunity, let us do good to all people, especially to those who belong to the family of believers" (Gal. 6:10, NIV).

Bill's family often kids him about being the kind of guy who could "fall into a sewer and come up with a ham sandwich." In Bill's childhood years, he did seem to get a lot of breaks, even in what appeared to be impossible situations. Just by being in the right place at the right time, he met the person who helped him with a scholarship to graduate school. When I was pregnant with our first child and needed to be home full-time, a job opened up for Bill just when we needed it. When our hearts were telling us God had more, a ministry opportunity opened up, and that ministry has continued to open other doors.

Opportunity

From watching Bill at close range, I think he has learned to recognize opportunity. Opportunity isn't always just good breaks. Opportunity often comes in adversity. The apostle Paul said in 1 Corinthians 16, "But I will tarry in Ephesus until Pentecost. For a great and effective door has opened to me, and there are many adversaries" (1 Cor. 16:8-9).

In his book *Creative Suffering,* Paul Tournier writes about the creativity inherent in deprivation and suffering. We see many practical examples of this. When Joseph was sold into slavery, he maintained his integrity, found

amazing opportunity, and went on to become a leader in Egypt. Esther, the beautiful young Jewish girl who became queen, used that opportunity to save her people.

Rather than see restrictions and limits, we can view a situation as a place with definition and possibilities. In publishing magazines, we have budgets we must work within; we know what we can spend for paper, printing, and staff. But rather than see a budget as a confining factor, we choose to see it as an opportunity for creativity, a forum for borders and definition from which to grow.

My (Nancie's) mother lived with very difficult circumstances, yet her life became a showplace of God's grace because she used what she had, where she was, to honor God. Living out on the Montana plains as a farmer's wife, she could have become frustrated and bitter with what may have looked like a dreary existence. Yet she made it a place of opportunity. With charm and humor she invested her gifts and energy in her family of seven children. She became a 4-H leader; she taught Sunday school. She used these opportunities to encourage others and teach God's Word to young people. Her influence is still felt today in the lives of many people. Mother used to tell us children, "Use obstacles as building blocks toward God."

We must pray that our children will have a godly perspective on opportunity. America is built on the concept of free enterprise—the idea of finding a need and filling it. But we and our children must learn to ask, "What is my ultimate goal in this opportunity?" We must pray that our children will see all of life as an opportunity to honor God, to live out His commandments.

Just before Moses died, he left this poignant plea with his people: "I command you today to love the Lord your God, to walk in His ways, and to keep His commandments, . . . I call heaven and earth as witnesses today against you, that I have set before you life and death, blessing and cursing; therefore choose life, that both you and your descendants may live" (Deut. 30:16, 19).

God has given each of us a precious commodity: our will. We can choose our responses to situations. Every day is a new day of opportunity, another fork in the road, a place to make big and small decisions that shape our lives.

I pray that my children will, first of all, be motivated to honor God with their dreams and plans. I pray that they will learn to recognize opportunities that come their way, even in difficult situations. I pray that they will have the courage to use every situation as an opportunity for God's glory.

R E F L E C T I O N

"Every morning is a fresh beginning. Every day the world is made new. Today is a new day. Today is my world made new. I have lived all my life up to this moment, to come to this day. This moment—this day—is as good as any moment in all eternity. I shall make of this day—each moment of this day— a heaven on earth. This is my day of opportunity."

Dan Custer

"When one door closes, another opens; but we often look so long and so regretfully upon the closed door that we do not see the one which has opened for us."

Alexander Graham Bell

FAMILY INTERACTION

1 Over a period of time, read with your family the story of Joseph (Gen. 37–50). Discuss the impact that Joseph's responses had on the various situations he was in:
- with his brothers (chapter 37)
- within Pharoah's house with Potiphar's wife (chapter 39)
- in prison (chapters 39–40)
- his dealings with Pharaoh and his rise to power (chapters 41)
- reuniting with his brothers (chapters 42–45).

2 Describe what possible scenarios could have occurred if Joseph had used these opportunities for revenge and selfishness. Apply the story of Joseph's life to your family, discussing actual opportunities you've had and how you've used them.

COMMUNICATING THE BLESSING

I pray for you, my child, that you will learn to recognize good opportunity and to resist evil opportunity. I pray that God will give you the wisdom to discern the difference.

MY PRAYER FOR MY CHILD

NAME _____ DATE _____

_____

_____

_____

FOLLOW-UP PRAYERS, ANSWERS, AND INSIGHTS

NAME _____ DATE _____

_____

_____

Opportunity

LORD, BLESS MY CHILD WITH . . .

ORIGINALITY

37

Don't copy the behavior and customs of this world, but be a new and different person.

Romans 12:2, TLB

PRAYER

Lord, we are all originals whom you have created. Help my child not to shrink from originality. Help my child not to fall prey to the false gods of glamour and fads. Help my child instead demonstrate new ideas and direction when circumstances demand it, to be himself or herself in spite of pressure to conform. Help me to encourage my child to enjoy being Your original masterpiece.

SCRIPTURE

"My frame was not hidden from you when I was made in the secret place. When I was woven together in the depths of the earth, your eyes saw my unformed body" (Ps. 139:15-16, NIV).

151

In a family setting, children naturally compare themselves to each other and compete with each other. It's a challenge for parents, especially if there are several children in the family, to encourage originality. Eric, our second oldest son, had a somewhat melancholy personality as a little guy. He would compare himself to his older brother, Jon, an outgoing enthusiast. Nothing made Eric happier than to know his big brother approved of him.

Riding in the car one day, Eric, about four years old at the time, was feeling a little insecure about himself. He had an idea how to bolster his self-esteem. He announced, "Whoever likes me, raise your hand!" We parents, of course, raised our hands, little Chris raised his hand, but Jon appeared oblivious, humming under his breath, staring out the window. Eric was devastated. "Mom! Jon won't raise his hand." Jon looked up with innocent blue eyes and belatedly raised his hand.

As our younger children came into the schools that their older siblings had been through, the teachers had a tendency to say, "Oh, there's another Carmichael" and expect them to play basketball and be in the music program. And they all did, to one degree or another, although two years of the trombone was all Eric could handle of instrumental music. (The rest of us agreed.)

It always frustrated us as parents to see that if one of the children had a specific talent, the others would back away from it, even if they were gifted in that area, because it was the other person's "talent." Chris and Andy are both gifted writers, yet somehow Andy hasn't yet claimed that as one of his strengths because that gift, he feels, belongs to Chris. The best we can do as parents is to encourage each of our children's originality.

Even in a family where the children seem alike at first glance, there are enormous differences. Each is unique. Parents have the responsibility of treating the kids alike but encouraging their uniqueness.

When Amy came along at age three from a Korean orphanage, we had a lot to learn about the originality of each child. After four athletic boys, I (Nancie) had it in my mind how Amy would be: She would love lacy, pink dresses, music, and books; in other words, she would be like me.

As we watched Amy's personality unfold, we began to realize she is an original. Amy doesn't like frilly dresses; she likes ones that are tailored, in plaids or blacks or reds. She loves baseball; in fact, the pajamas she wore when she arrived at the Sea-Tac International

Airport from Korea had baseballs on them. Amy expresses a tender compassion toward the underdog, the disadvantaged; she knows how it feels. We've learned a lot about originality from Amy. She is one of God's gifts to our family.

Proverbs 22:6 says, "Train up a child in the way he should go." In *The Amplified Bible* it says, "In keeping with his . . . bent." Each child has a natural bent, a key. Sometimes it takes a bit of study and waiting to discover what each child's key is. What makes this child happy? What motivates this child? When does this child seem to come alive? Watch for the key to your child's originality. When you find it, encourage it and help it come into full bloom.

Each of us is a unique masterpiece developed by our Creator. How painful it is to have someone close to us—especially a parent—not see the masterpiece and, instead, try to change it. If we were to go into the National Gallery of Art and try to touch up some of those masterpieces with a gallon of paint, we would be dragged out of there in a hurry. And yet we do that at times to our children. We try to change who they are. We are called as parents to correct, discipline, and disciple our children in the Lord, but above all we must love them. And loving them means we must *see* them as God has made them: originals.

I pray that my children will realize that no one else in the entire world is like them and that God has given each of them individual gifts and has called them to individual work in His kingdom. I pray that they will discover who they are in Christ and will serve Him wholeheartedly with their uniqueness.

REFLECTION

*"We were given to one another by the Lord of the Body—
because each one of us has a unique something to contribute—
a piece of the divine puzzle no one else on earth can supply."*

Charles Swindoll, *Come before Winter*

*"We are not hen's eggs, or bananas,
or clothespins, to be counted off by the dozen.
Down to the last detail we are all different.
Everyone has his own fingerprints.
Recognize and rejoice in that endless variety."*

Charles R. Brown, "Who Are We?"

FAMILY INTERACTION

1 Ask your child, "What are three of your greatest strengths?" Affirm your child's list and add three more strengths that you see in him or her.

2 Ask your child, "What are three of your greatest weaknesses?"

3 Ask your child, "What do you like about yourself? What would you change about yourself?"

4 Write responses to these things, as a way of self-discovery (adapted from A. W. Tozer):

- What do I want most?
- What do I think about most?
- What do I do with my leisure time?

- Whose company do I enjoy?
- Whom and what do I admire?
- What makes me laugh?

COMMUNICATING THE BLESSING

I pray for you, my child, that you will be you. God created you, and the best fulfillment of His will is for you to be all that He wants for you. I pray that you will have the maturity to realize you cannot compare yourself to others. You are an original. Respond to God, the Creator of the masterpiece, in the deepest part of your being.

MY PRAYER FOR MY CHILD

NAME _____ DATE _____

_____

_____

_____

FOLLOW-UP PRAYERS, ANSWERS, AND INSIGHTS

NAME _____ DATE _____

_____

_____

LORD, BLESS MY CHILD WITH . . .

PEACE

38

Peace I leave with you, My peace I give to you; not as the world gives do I give to you.

J o h n   1 4 : 2 7

P R A Y E R

Lord, we see more hatred and discord than ever. Remind us that real peace only comes from You. I pray You will give my child that inner calm that passes understanding, that wonderful sense that You are there, that You know all things, and that You are in control.

S C R I P T U R E

"You will keep him in perfect peace, whose mind is stayed on You, because he trusts in You" (Isa. 26:3).

Our family Christmas photo this year is a snapshot of our children on the beach at the Cayman Islands, our "trip of a lifetime." I had ordered photo cards that read, "Wishing you a world of peace." I didn't notice the significance of that greeting until I got the photo cards back. The top of the photo shows dark storm clouds brewing, but the sun is shining directly down on our kids. The looks on their faces are pure joy and peace. Conflict and the storms of life inevitably come.

Conflict appears in our relationships and in professional situations. We sense the cultural war raging in our society now, with the clash of values becoming increasingly clear.

More real to us are the conflicts that can rage inside us: Regret, guilt, shame, fear, and resentment can destroy inner peace. Jesus never promised an absence of conflict or problems, but He did promise peace: "Peace I leave with you, My peace I give to you; not as the world gives do I give to you. Let not your heart be troubled, neither let it be afraid" (John 14:27).

A very real enemy of peace is fear. We are threatened and afraid of things that are different from us. A. W. Tozer, in *The Knowledge of the Holy*, writes,

Fear is the painful emotion that arises at the thought that we may be harmed or made to suffer. This fear persists while we are subject to the will of someone who does not desire our well-being. The moment we come under the protection of one of good will, fear is cast out. A child lost in a crowded store is full of fear because it sees the strangers around it as enemies. In its mother's arms a moment later all the terror subsides. The known good will of the mother casts out fear. . . . To know that love is of God and to enter into the secret place leaning on the arm of the Beloved—this and only this can cast out fear.

Nancie's brother, Joe Pearson, is a pastor in Montana. Recently he had the privilege of baptizing his youngest daughter, Noel, age eight. He had gone over the doctrine of water baptism with Noel thoroughly, but he still wasn't entirely sure she comprehended the full meaning. But in her quiet way, Noel was determined it was time for her to be baptized. At the baptismal service, Joe asked her in front of the congregation, "Noel, what does being baptized mean to you?" Noel, a shy child who tends to be fearful, convinced him she was ready when she responded emphatically, "Dad, it means *no fear!*"

Jesus is our peace. He took our sin on Himself at the Cross, and we can plunge into His presence, casting our care and sin on His mercy and grace. "For He Himself is our peace, who has made both one, and has broken down the middle wall of separation. . . . And He came and preached peace to you who were afar off and to those who were near" (Eph. 2:14, 17).

I pray that my children will know the peace that passes understanding in the midst of life with all its storms. I pray that they will know intimately the Prince of Peace, Jesus, who is able to keep them sheltered, covered by His peace as they keep their mind focused on Him.

R E F L E C T I O N

"Peace is the ability to stay calm in spite of the panic of unpleasant circumstances."

Charles Swindoll, *Stress Fractures*

"My Father, so seldom do I feel the rich and unshakable peace of heaven, which You promised to me. Is it because I am so often concerned with pleasing others— afraid they'll think poorly of me? Do I work too hard, as if it's my job, to make certain people happy?"

Amy Carmichael, *You Are My Hiding Place*

"The sum of the whole matter is this, that our civilization cannot survive materially unless it is redeemed spiritually. It can be saved only by becoming permeated with the spirit of Christ and being made free and happy by the practices which spring out of that spirit. Only thus can discontent be driven out and all the shadows lifted from the road ahead."

Woodrow Wilson

FAMILY INTERACTION

1 Read Matthew 11:29. Ask your child, "What does it mean to have rest for your soul?"

2 Rent a video such as *The Hiding Place*. Better yet, read the book with your child. Discuss how Corrie ten Boom's family could experience peace in the midst of such awful times.

3 Read Isaiah 40:11. Ask your child, "What does it mean to be carried by God?"

4 When the moment is right, ask your child, "Do you have God's peace in you now? If not, why not?" An excellent book on this essential quality is Billy Graham's book *Peace with God*.

COMMUNICATING THE BLESSING

I pray for you, my child, that you have peace. It is doubtful you will ever witness world peace until Jesus returns, but you can experience His peace in an amazing capacity through His power and joy within you. I pray that you will find your perfect peace in Him.

MY PRAYER FOR MY CHILD

NAME _____ DATE _____

_____

_____

_____

FOLLOW-UP PRAYERS, ANSWERS, AND INSIGHTS

NAME _____ DATE _____

_____

_____

_____

LORD, BLESS MY CHILD WITH . . .

SAFETY

39

For I know whom I have believed and am persuaded that

He is able to keep what I have committed to Him until that Day.

2 Timothy 1:12

PRAYER

Lord, You know how I yearn for my children's safety, their best. O holy Father, I pray for my children's *physical safety,* that they would be kept from harm's way. I pray for their *emotional safety,* that their minds would be garrisoned from mental stress and illness. But most of all, I pray for their *spiritual safety,* that they would be kept in You—the ultimate safe place.

SCRIPTURE

"In the shelter of your presence you hide them from the intrigues of men; in your dwelling you keep them safe" (Ps. 31:20, NIV).

Almost twenty years ago, when Jon was six, Eric was four, and Chris was two, I (Nancie) sat in their bedroom to pray with them before they went to sleep. The next day was Jon's first day at school. He was excited; I was filled with dread. How could I give this precious child to strangers? I tried not to show my own fear because Jon was nervous about riding the school bus. I already envisioned how he would look in front of the house the next morning: new jeans and navy blue windbreaker, his pink name tag around his neck, his white-blond hair neatly combed, looking for all the world like a lamb being led to slaughter. I silently wondered, *Whose idea was it to have pink name tags, anyway? Older boys might tease him.*

"Boys," I told them—more for my sake than theirs—"remember, you have guardian angels. The Bible says that the angel of the Lord camps around those who fear Him. Psalm 91:11 says, 'For He shall give His angels charge over you, to keep you in all your ways.' We can't see the angels because they're invisible. But they're very real. In fact, I saw my guardian angel one time."

"You did?" I had their attention. And so I told them. . . .

I was about nine years old when I awoke one night to see someone sitting on my bed. I knew instinctively he was an angel. I stared at him, this awesome-looking creature, with a full, curly head of hair, wearing a flowing robe of some kind. I lay frozen, staring in fascinated terror. My mother always left the stove light on in the kitchen so that some light would filter into the bedrooms. In the soft light I could see him plainly. He was as real as my two sisters, who were sleeping soundly in the same room with me. I breathed shallowly, not wanting him to know I was awake. Then he turned his head and looked at me. I immediately closed my eyes, pretending to be asleep. And I did go to sleep. When I told my family the next morning, they nodded and smiled, but I think they thought I was dreaming. I wasn't. The encounter is still real and vivid to me.

I finished telling the story, then sang to them, "All day, all night, angels watchin' over me." Just as I was tucking them in, Bill came in the door from a meeting at the church. He poked his head in the bedroom. "I've got a surprise for you guys." He held three large, ornately decorated angel cookies, one for each of the boys. "Alice from the church made these for you."

Angel cookies? Why would Alice make angel cookies for our sons in *September?*

Jon's assessment: "Hey, God is saying, `You really do have guardian angels!'"

Now, years later, we ponder how often we've prayed for safety for our children. And we remember how He has shown Himself to be Immanuel, "God with us," so many times. In these days when we hear heartbreaking stories of abused children, we wonder, *How can this happen? What great evil causes adults to harm and exploit children? How can God allow these things to be?* And yet we know that God has given us the power of choice that carries with it enormous consequences.

Ultimately, we know we must trust God and trust His keeping power, knowing that "whether we live or die, we are the Lord's"

(Rom. 14:8). It seems that almost from a child's first breath, we parents are constantly called on to let go. It doesn't matter if it's the first time we get a baby-sitter or the first time our child comes home with a driver's license, we have an overwhelming desire to protect our children and to keep them safe. The thought that our children could be harmed is indeed a parent's worst nightmare. But in this vulnerable area of trust for us parents, we are reminded that the ultimate safe place is in God's hands. Proverbs 18:10 says, "The name of the Lord is a strong tower; the righteous run to it and are safe."

I pray that my children will be kept safe, safe from physical harm and especially safe from the evil one, who would destroy. I pray that my children will have that wonderful sense of being cradled by God, even in the stormy times of their lives, that they will run to the shelter of the Lord's presence for refuge.

R E F L E C T I O N

"Often we fear giving up our treasures to the Lord out of fear for their safety. . . .
Our Lord came not to destroy, but to save.
Everything is safe which we commit to Him."

A . W . Tozer

"I have held many things in my hands and have lost them all;
but that which I have committed to God, that I still possess."

Martin Luther

FAMILY INTERACTION

1 Discuss what it means to feel safe.

2 What makes home safe physically and emotionally?

3 Discuss with your family (keeping in mind age-appropriate situations) how to keep safe without living in fear.

COMMUNICATING THE BLESSING

I pray for you, my child, that you will be blessed with safety. I love you so much and do not want you to be in pain or suffering or to be exploited in any way. But most of all, I pray that you will be kept safe from the evil one and kept in our Father's hands.

MY PRAYER FOR MY CHILD

NAME _____ DATE _____

_____

_____

_____

_____

FOLLOW-UP PRAYERS, ANSWERS, AND INSIGHTS

NAME _____ DATE _____

_____

_____

_____

Safety

LORD, HELP MY CHILD TO DESIRE TO . . .

Be Available to God

Be Still

Be Teachable

Honor Others

Make Good Choices

Remember God's Goodness

Seek Wisdom

PART 4

AVAILABLE TO GOD

40

Then Jesus said to them, "Follow Me, and I will make you become fishers of men."

They immediately left their nets and followed Him.

Mark 1:17-18

PRAYER

As Samuel responded to you, Lord, by saying, "Speak, for Your servant hears"; as Isaiah responded, "Here am I! Send me"; as Saul was transformed into the apostle Paul so also may my child be available to hear Your voice and do Your bidding. Lord, give my child a willingness and eagerness to do whatever You ask. Lord, help me reflect Your availability by being available to my children.

SCRIPTURE

"And David said, 'What have I done now? Is there not a cause? . . . Let no man's heart fail because of him; your servant will go and fight with this Philistine'" (1 Sam. 17:29, 32).

Last September I (Nancie) took a nasty fall between our boat and the dock, fracturing and partially dislocating my shoulder. The injury required surgery and bed rest for a while. You need to know that I am not the kind of mom who sits down much at home. I always see work to do, and true to my Martha nature, I'm always buzzing about. But for a time I sat on the family-room sofa, pillows propped under and around me as I tried to get comfortable. What remains with me about that time are my children's reactions to me.

They were delighted to see their mother sitting down on their turf, the family-room sofa. I never, but *never* sat there. I vacuumed it, picked up stray kernels of popcorn on it, but I never *sat* there. I realized with a pang that I was now truly available to them—not to do things for them but to talk with them. I was not distracted by anything else, and it was very sweet to be together with no agenda other than to be together. We were truly available to one another, listening to one another.

How do we listen to God so that we are available to Him? One four-year-old girl sat on her mother's lap. "I hear Jesus, Mommy," she said, pressing her head close to her mother's heart.

"And what is He saying?" the mother smiled.

The little girl listened carefully, then responded, "I think He's making coffee."

What keeps us from being available to God? Our hearts get divided. Like Martha, we become distracted—even by serving Jesus, when all He wants from us is for us to sit down, to listen to Him with an undivided heart. Maybe we need to have "coffee" with God. Being in His presence, studying the Scriptures, and being aware of Him are how we learn to cultivate the sound of His voice. We need to have our work come out of this quiet time with God. Our "doing" then reflects the "being," and it is so much more effective. How do we cultivate in our children this attitude of being available?

It comes through modeling. Are we ourselves available to God? Do our children see us in His presence with the Word and in prayer?

I (Bill) remember as a child when my family was considering a move, and I watched as my father prayed about the decision. This modeled availability for me: Is this what God wants for us and for our family? Being available is giving God first option on our lives.

Our priorities also tell our children how to be

available to God. Do they see us give priority to worship, to work on church committees, to giving financially to God's work, to offering hospitality, to showing acts of kindness to those in need?

Immediate needs, the "tyranny of the urgent" will try to dominate our lives. Even in writing this book, a wonderful project that we both want to do, so many things crowd in. We need to contact a repairman about the roof. A business associate calls and needs to meet for lunch. The house needs to be cleaned. The phone is ringing. In order to write the book, we have carved some time away to finish this project.

We've had to pull away from our lives to be available to God's voice.

"Here I am, Lord," means just that. We are here, waiting, open to His agenda, loving Him with all our hearts, souls, minds, and bodies. We are willing to take a risk, to be inconvenienced to follow Him.

I pray that my children will be available to the Lord, knowing that in Him there is safety, purpose, and the greatest fulfillment humanly possible. I pray that they will give their attention completely to God and His plan for their lives.

R E F L E C T I O N

"The more we receive in our silent prayer, the more we can give in our active life. Silence gives us a new way of looking at everything. We need this silence in order to touch souls. Jesus is always waiting for us in silence. Because we cannot see Christ, we cannot express our love to Him in person. But our neighbor we can see, and we can do for him or her what we would love to do for Jesus if He were visible. Let us be open to God so that he can use us. Let us put love into our actions, beginning in the family, in the neighborhood, in the street."

Mother Teresa, *The Love of Christ*

"The ideal gift is . . . yourself. Give an hour of your time. Give a note of encouragement. Give a hug of affirmation. Give a visit of mercy. Give a meal you prepared. Give a word of compassion. Give a deed of kindness."

Charles Swindoll, *The Quest for Character*

"The measure of a life, after all, is not its duration but its donation."

Corrie ten Boom

FAMILY INTERACTION

1 Read 1 Samuel 3 from *The Living Bible,* and tell this story to your child in your own words. Wait for their questions or response.

2 Play a game with your child. Tell your child that from time to time during the week, you will call his or her name once. If your child responds quickly, without having to be called again, he or she will get a coin, a small gift, sweets, a fun thing to do, etc. When your child comes in response to your call, discuss the value of being available to hear God's voice and responding quickly, just as he or she did when you called.

3 Ask your child, "How do we hear God's voice?" Possible answers include after prayer, while listening quietly, through Scripture, at church, and through circumstances and events of life.

COMMUNICATING THE BLESSING

I pray for you, my child, that you will be available to God. When you were a young child, we dedicated you to God. Our desire, as your parents, is that you will be clay in the Master's hands, shaped into a vessel of honor for His kingdom, power, and glory.

MY PRAYER FOR MY CHILD

NAME _____ DATE _____

_____

_____

FOLLOW-UP PRAYERS, ANSWERS, AND INSIGHTS

NAME _____ DATE _____

_____

_____

LORD, HELP MY CHILD TO DESIRE TO . . .

Be Still

41

Be still, and know that I am God; I will be exalted among the nations,

I will be exalted in the earth!

Psalm 46:10

PRAYER

O Father, You know how hard it is for me to be still. But I know how important it is for me to learn to be still because it is in the stillness that I come to know You. The greatest threat to being still is our frenetic schedules. I see it in my child's life too, a child already so busy and scheduled. I pray that my child will be blessed by having time to be *still,* to listen for Your voice, to know You. Help all of us to be sensitive to opportunities to be still.

"Truly my soul silently waits for God; from Him comes my salvation. He only is my rock and my salvation; He is my defense; I shall not be greatly moved" (Ps. 62:1-2).

The wonderful part of growing up on a farm in Montana is being out in the country with many places to explore and play. When I (Nancie) was a girl, I often had a secret place. Sometimes it was in the hayloft of the old barn. Once it was in a grove of willow trees at the end of a lane. Then there was the time I used a tree house my brother built behind the house until he decided to tear it down for something else. If a granary was empty, it made a great secret place. I can still see in my mind's eye the shafts of light streaming in from the high windows of the granary as I swung on the iron bars that crisscrossed the inside of the storage building. I could bolt the door from the inside, and no one could get in without my permission. When my little brothers and sisters found out about my secret place, I had to find a new one. It had to be *my* place, and mine alone.

In this day of invasive media and noise, it is absolutely vital that our children learn the value of being alone, being still. Sometimes our children just need to be alone to feel the wind on their faces and see the swallows wheeling against the sky, to think about God, to talk to Him, and to spin dreams for the future.

Last spring when our sons were home from college for break, Chris took the dogs and me on a romp through the Forest Service property behind our house. "I want to show you a place," he said. It took some meandering, but we found it: an old, ramshackle log cabin. He showed me the door he and his brother made to get in. "We used to come here and play," he reminisced. Chris crawled into the cabin, the old musty pine needles looking as if they hadn't been disturbed in years. It was amazing to think that all the time we parents had been back at the house trying to keep all the plates spinning, our boys had retreated to a place we knew nothing about. It was a good feeling to know they had secret places too.

In this world with so much coming at us, it is so important for our children to be still, to know God's voice. The Hebrew word for a secret place is *sether,* meaning a covering, a hiding place. Close to our house is a small lake surrounded by aspen trees. On clear days, when the lake is still, the reflection of the trees on the lake is so perfect that I can hardly tell where the reflection begins. When we are like that lake, still in God's presence, we can more clearly reflect Him. We can become still by finding that hiding place, that secret place where we can meet God. Jesus said, "When you pray, go into your room, and when you have shut your door, pray to your Father who is in the secret place" (Matt. 6:6).

Perhaps we are afraid to be still because we don't like the sound of our own emptiness or pain or confusion. But it is precisely in our weaknesses that God makes Himself known to us as He restores us, forgives us, renews our strength, guides us, and convicts us of what we need to change. In his book *A Fresh Encounter,* Henry Blackaby observes that our culture is conditioned to get information and be entertained. Often we come to God on those terms. What really changes us is *an encounter* with God, like the kind Isaiah had

(Isa. 6). When we meet God, we see His holiness, and He changes us.

How do we help our children desire to be still and listen to God? We can encourage them by our own example, first of all. Do they see us spending time with God? Do they see us retreat from the noises within and without so that we can hear God's voice more clearly? Then we can give them some tools to lead them into stillness: devotional materials, Bibles, and journals in which they can record their thoughts and prayers. And we can pray that they will find secret places to be still before God.

I pray that my children will desire to be still in God's presence, that they will dig down deep into the truths of God's Word for themselves. I pray that they will learn the value of meditating on Scripture, of letting the Holy Spirit speak through the Word to the quiet of their being. I pray that in the clatter and din of their noisy lives, they will find quiet places for God to speak.

R E F L E C T I O N

"Where do you go to find enough stillness to rediscover that God is God? Where do you turn when your days and nights start running together?"

Charles Swindoll, *Come before Winter*

"A quiet place is a good place to find out God's angle on any problem."

Jeanette Oke, *Once upon a Summer*

"He who waits for God loses no time."

Anonymous

FAMILY INTERACTION

1 Encourage your child to be still, to go away if necessary, in order to have quiet time with God.

2 Agree with your other family members to have some specific times when no television, radio, or stereo will be on in your home.

COMMUNICATING THE BLESSING

I pray for you, my child, to desire to be still and listen quietly to God. He often speaks in a still, small voice that takes patience and practice to hear. I pray that you will learn the art of quiet time, of becoming comfortable with silence. Both are rare these days and especially hard for young people, but they are essential to knowing God in a deeper way.

MY PRAYER FOR MY CHILD

NAME _____ DATE _____

_____

_____

_____

_____

FOLLOW-UP PRAYERS, ANSWERS, AND INSIGHTS

NAME _____ DATE _____

_____

_____

_____

LORD, HELP MY CHILD TO DESIRE TO BE . . .

TEACHABLE

42

Incline your ear, and come to Me. Hear, and your soul shall live.

Isaiah 55:3

PRAYER

Thank You, Lord, for providing people to whom I can be accountable. I pray that my child will have trusted people to turn to, that he or she will be willing to give an account to those in authority. Help my child realize that to have a teachable spirit is a healthy way to stay on track and avoid getting derailed into dishonesty, a misuse of power, or a diffusion of goals.

SCRIPTURE

"My son, give attention to my words; incline your ear to my sayings. Do not let them depart from your eyes; keep them in the midst of your heart; for they are life to those who find them, and health to all their flesh. Keep your heart with all diligence, for out of it spring the issues of life" (Prov. 4:20-23).

No teacher can teach without pupils. To be subject to someone else, we must be submissive, want to know, become willing to be taught.

When I (Nancie) was a girl, I took piano lessons. My teacher, Mrs. Bain, stressed to her students the importance of having a teachable spirit. It was key to knowing how to sight-read, how to play Bach the way he intended it, how to to play Chopin the way it deserved to be played. If I listened to the metronome, got my timing right, and obeyed the notes and expression marks, I could become successful. At the time, I didn't fully understand why Mrs. Bain spoke so often of having a teachable spirit, but now as I enjoy playing the piano and helping our own children with music, I am grateful I learned.

Our daughter, Amy, started seventh grade this year, and shortly after school started, she came home quite upset. "I hate math," she stormed. "I'll never get it!" We tried to understand what she was learning, and frankly, it was over our heads too. Her teacher said she would be willing to help Amy at noon if she would take the time to go in and ask for help. Due to the patient persistence of her teacher, Amy became willing to be taught; and she did learn. In fact, she became the Student of the Month in her

grade for math! But to be willing to learn, she had to admit she didn't understand it, and she had to be willing to be taught.

There is an element of humility in being teachable. When Bill was in charge of publishing the magazines and would need to hire a new person, he would always tell him or her, "Don't be afraid to ask questions. There are no dumb questions. I will worry if you *don't* ask questions."

To have a child with a teachable spirit, we must somehow reach the heart of the child. When our children were babies, we sometimes dipped their pacifier in a bit of honey so they would take the pacifier. The Psalms remind us, "Oh, that My people would listen to Me, that Israel would walk in My ways. . . . [I] would have fed them also with the finest of wheat; and with honey from the rock I would have satisfied you" (Ps. 81:13, 16). How we long for our children to be teachable in the things of God. We want them to see that if they develop a teachable spirit, God will feed them with the finest of wheat and with honey from the rock.

The apostle Paul in his youth sat at the feet of the great teacher Gamaliel. In turn, Paul taught Timothy, calling him "a true son in

Teachable

the faith" (1 Tim. 1:2). He urged Timothy, "Continue in the things which you have learned and been assured of, knowing from whom you have learned them, and that from childhood you have known the Holy Scriptures, which are able to make you wise for salvation through faith which is in Christ Jesus" (2 Tim. 3:14-15).

We can give our children no greater gift than a love for the Scriptures, for the things of God. We can sweeten the learning with "honey"—not cramming it down our chil-dren's throats in a legalistic manner, but teaching with love and enthusiasm. We can make sure our children's Christian education is a positive experience, and in their forma-tive years, we can help them memorize Scripture. God's Word has a lifelong, pro-found impact.

I pray that my children will have teachable spirits, especially toward the things of God. I pray that they will have the courage to admit when they don't know something and the desire to make learning a lifelong quest.

R E F L E C T I O N

"Education . . . It is not teaching the youth the shapes of letters and the tricks of numbers, and then leaving them to turn their arithmetic to roguery, and their literature to lust. It means, on the contrary, training them into the perfect exercise and kingly continence of their bodies and souls. It is a painful, continual, and difficult work to be done by kindness, by watching, by warning, by precept, and by praise, but above all—by example."

John Ruskin

"Should God place you on His anvil, be thankful. It means he thinks you're still worth reshaping."

Max Lucado, *On the Anvil*

F A M I L Y   I N T E R A C T I O N

1 Decide as a family to learn something new, something you've never done before, such as a sport or a game. Study the rules and practice it until you learn it. Discuss the elements necessary for you to master this new skill or sport.

Teachable

2 Later, read 2 Timothy 1:5. Ask your child, "What does this tell us about how Timothy was taught in his early years?"

3 Read 1 Timothy 4:12-16. Ask your child, "What does this tell us about how God views your potential to grow and develop, even though you are young?"

4 Tell your family about a time that you learned something that gave you great satisfaction. Ask your child, "What new thing would you really like to learn? How can you learn that new skill? How can we help?"

COMMUNICATING THE BLESSING

I pray for you, my child, to desire to be teachable. As a parent, I am your first teacher. Later, many others will teach you. I pray that you will welcome teaching and accountability. Often those in authority will not demand this of you, but when you open your heart to learn from those who can teach you, you are on a pathway to wisdom. A willingness to learn is an important first step to many opportunities.

MY PRAYER FOR MY CHILD

NAME _____ DATE _____

_____

_____

_____

FOLLOW-UP PRAYERS, ANSWERS, AND INSIGHTS

NAME _____ DATE _____

_____

_____

_____

Teachable

HONOR OTHERS

43

Honor and majesty are before Him; strength and beauty are in His sanctuary.

Psalm 96:6

PRAYER

Lord, I pray that You bless my child with a desire to honor others, to show respect, to cherish ideals. Help my child to honor You first, to keep a day of rest for You, to honor himself or herself as a temple of the Holy Spirit, and to remember the things that matter.

SCRIPTURE

"Honor your father and mother, that you may have a long, good life in the land the Lord your God will give you" (Exod. 20:12, TLB).

"Honor the Lord with your possessions, and with the firstfruits of all your increase" (Prov. 3:9).

Honor really means *living* what is important. Honor is an elusive quality that is best caught, not taught. Our children will honor and respect what we honor and respect. They tend ultimately to honor those traditions and ideals that we honor by our example. In our fast-paced lifestyle with its emphasis on winning, too often the end justifies the means. Honor can get lost.

I (Bill) have learned to enjoy playing golf with my sons. Our sons learned to play golf at a nearby course where they have worked since they were small. One thing I like about golf is that it is a game of honor, a game long considered a gentleman's sport. The essence of the rules of golf is dependent on an unwritten code of honor. The other thing I like about the rules of golf is that others can give you grace that, according to the rules, you cannot give to yourself. If I have a questionable lie, I can consult with the other players. If they agree that I can take a free drop from an unnatural hazard or other difficulties, then I may move my ball. But it takes their agreement and consent to prevent a violation of the rules. I know of no other game where the temptation to cheat—to "fluff up" a bad lie, to move the ball a few inches from under a tree to get a better angle when no one is looking, or to forget about a small duff swing

when recording your score—is so strong. But to violate the rules—even if no one knows— is to lose self-respect.

It's that way in life too. The temptation is strong to tell the little white lie, to "forget" to report a cash transaction on an income-tax report, to keep the extra change when a clerk makes a mistake. But honor is more than honesty. While honor, in one sense, is being true to one's inner self, honor is also tied to the value we give to others: our children, our parents, our spouse, our government and country, and God. Honor means giving respect because it is due. One of *Webster's* definitions of *honor* is "personal integrity maintained without legal or other obligation."

Honor becomes our code for life. Honor decides what things we are willing to die for. There has never been someone who committed treason who also had a code of honor. Likewise, there have been many who have lost their lives while defending the honor of some ideal larger than themselves.

Sometimes we have the mistaken notion that we give honor only when it benefits us. But giving the gift of honor means to give respect to whomever or to whatever is due that respect. Our children learn to honor what we honor. Do we honor our own parents? Do we honor truth? Do we honor the Lord's Day? Do we honor the pastors in our church and the preaching of God's Word? Do we honor the laws of the land? Do we honor flag and country? Do we honor God with our tithes and offerings? Do we honor true heroes of our country and of the faith?

Most important, we can show our children what it means to honor by honoring them as unique individuals, by showing them unconditional love and care, by listening to them as if they were the most important people in the world.

I pray that my children will desire to honor others. Help my children see that a code of honor is a lovingly crafted, invisible structure on which to build a God-honoring life. Help me as their parent to practice honoring other people.

R E F L E C T I O N

"Honor is a decision we make to place high value, worth, and importance on another person by viewing him or her as a priceless gift and granting him or her a position in our lives worthy of great respect; and love involves putting that decision into action."

Gary Smalley and John Trent, *The Gift of Honor*

"If you wish others to respect you, you must show respect for them. For twenty days, approach everyone you meet, irrespective of his station in life, as if he or she were the most important person in the world. Everyone wants to feel that he counts for something and is important to someone. Invariably, people will give their love, respect, and attention to the person who fills that need."

Ari Kiev

F A M I L Y   I N T E R A C T I O N

1 Discuss memorials, perhaps the Vietnam Veterans Memorial. Ask your child, "What are you willing to die for?" Share with your child your response to the same question.

2 Ask your child, "What do you honor, respect, or hold high?" Share your response to the same question.

3 Ask your child, "How do showing respect for the flag, standing when we sing the national anthem, and standing when we read the Bible in church help to show honor?"

4 Ask your child, "How can using good manners show honor?"

COMMUNICATING THE BLESSING

I pray for you, my child, that you would live a life of honor. May you understand what it means first of all to honor God, His Word, and truth. And out of that foundation, may you view your own life and others' lives with a sense of honor.

MY PRAYER FOR MY CHILD

NAME _____ DATE _____

_____

_____

_____

_____

_____

FOLLOW-UP PRAYERS, ANSWERS, AND INSIGHTS

NAME _____ DATE _____

_____

_____

_____

_____

Honor Others

GOOD CHOICES

44

I call heaven and earth as witnesses today against you, that I have set before you life and death, blessing and cursing; therefore choose life, that both you and your descendants may live; that you may love the Lord your God, that you may obey His voice, and that you may cling to Him, for He is your life and the length of your days.

Deuteronomy 30:19-20

PRAYER

Lord, thank You for giving us the precious ability to make choices. The array of choices we have today is overwhelming. Sometimes we are tempted to choose the path of least resistance, of greatest convenience, of strongest appeal. I pray that my child will desire to make life-giving, wholesome choices. I pray that my child will look to You and Your Word as the basis for wise choices.

"Choose for yourselves this day whom you will serve, whether the gods which your fathers served that were on the other side of the River, or the gods of the Amorites, in whose land you dwell. But as for me and my house, we will serve the Lord" (Josh. 24:15).

Many things change. Some things never change, such as the power of choice and how it affects out lives. Not long ago, Bill and I stood before the student body of the college we had attended twenty-five years earlier. Two of our sons were students there, and Eric, dressed in Bermuda shorts, introduced us as speakers for the day. When we had been at this college as students—in the late 1960s— boys sat on one side of the chapel, and girls on the other. Shorts were certainly not allowed.

As we sat in chapel that day, I realized again how powerful are the choices we make, especially when we are in the teen and college years. The choices made then have far-reaching effects on our lives.

I made a very important choice on that campus: At an altar in a small chapel, God and I had a confrontation, and God won. It was the first of many altars at which I knelt. In each new place, after every choice—marriage, work, motherhood, loss—I have had an opportunity to make Jesus Lord of my life.

At an early age, Bill also made the all-important choice to follow God. But we have found that this cornerstone choice is tested over and over. How do I respond to this situation? What should my attitude be? Do I take time to read the Bible and pray this morning? These choices influence how the rest of our lives are played out. Jesus said in Matthew 6:24, "No one can serve two masters; for either he will hate the one and love the other, or else he will be loyal to the one and despise the other. You cannot serve God and mammon."

How important it is to pray that our children will make good choices. We older adults have experiences that give us a broader perspective on life, and it is so tempting to give advice about what our children should do. If they would only listen to us, we could save them a lot of trouble! But, like their parents, they often need to find their way on their own. We have not always made the right choices. God's mercy and grace covers us, though, and it never fails to amaze us that even when we've made poor choices, the instant we turn our hearts toward Him, He meets us.

Good Choices

We are comforted by the model of the Prodigal Son in Luke 15, and although he made choices that were based upon shortsightedness and self-ishness, his father allowed him to go. When he came to his senses and realized his poor choices had ruined his life, he went back home to his father's open arms. We do not want our children to be like that son, but we cannot make their choices for them.

Bill has often stressed to us as a family that although we are perfect and we often make mistakes, we try to aim for the bull's-eye: Sometimes we are a little off target, but we keep aiming and get to the right place eventually. Our children (now in their teens and early twenties) are in the critical years when their choices are most powerful. They are choosing friends, colleges, life occupations, and spouses. We stand back and watch and pray. We sometimes have the urge to choose for them, thinking if they follow our advice, they will avoid trouble.

The really important choices in life—the choice to believe in Jesus Christ as one's personal Savior, to keep learning from the Word, to say yes to God, regardless—shape all the other choices we will make throughout life.

I pray my children will make, first of all, the all-important choice to follow Christ. I pray that as their lives unfold, their choices flow from having God as Lord of their lives.

R E F L E C T I O N

"We must all choose whether we will obey the gospel or turn away in unbelief and reject its authority. Our choice is our own, but the consequences of the choice have already been determined by the sovereign will of God, and from this there is no appeal."

A. W. Tozer, *The Knowledge of the Holy*

"Somewhere deep down we know that in the final analysis we do decide things and that even our decisions to let someone else decide are really our decisions."

Harvey G. Cox, *On Not Leaving It to the Snake*

F A M I L Y   I N T E R A C T I O N

1 Take out your old yearbooks and your child's baby books and other scrapbooks. Discuss with your child the effect that certain choices had on your life: what subjects you took, what

sports you played, whom you dated, whom you married, which college you attended. Ask your child to look at his or her scrapbooks and talk about the results of choices he or she has made.

2 Ask different family members to share what choices they are currently making and how it is affecting their lives now. Talk together about what impact these choices may have on their future as well as on the future of the other family members.

3 Read 1 Kings 18–20. Ask your child, "How did the choices these people—Elijah, Elisha, Ahab, and Jezebel—affect their lives?" See especially 1 Kings 18:21. Talk about this choice and its consequences.

COMMUNICATING THE BLESSING

I pray for you, my child, that you will make good choices. I pray, first of all, that you will choose to follow and serve God before all other gods. I pray that out of this all-important choice, you will make choices that not only will help you have a healthy, well-balanced, and meaningful life but also will bring meaning to other people's lives.

MY PRAYER FOR MY CHILD

NAME _____ DATE _____

_____

_____

_____

FOLLOW-UP PRAYERS, ANSWERS, AND INSIGHTS

NAME _____ DATE _____

_____

_____

_____

LORD, HELP MY CHILD TO DESIRE TO REMEMBER . . .

GOD'S GOODNESS

45

I call to remembrance my song in the night; I meditate within my heart,

and my spirit makes diligent search.

Psalm 77:6

PRAYER

God, we all too easily remember hurts, injustices, insults, and pain. Yet You have overwhelmed us with good things. I pray that my child will be blessed by remembering *tangible evidence* of Your intervention in his or her life. I pray that my child will be blessed by remembering Your goodness and faithfulness. Help us to celebrate as we remember Your dealings with us.

SCRIPTURE

"Oh, how great is Your goodness, which You have laid up for those who fear You, which You have prepared for those who trust in You in the presence of the sons of men! You shall hide them in the secret place of Your presence from the plots of man; You shall keep them secretly in a pavilion from the strife of tongues" (Ps. 31:19-20).

Reminders of God's goodness are all around us. Holidays and special family celebrations are wonderful opportunities to celebrate God's goodness to us. We recently celebrated the holidays, and it was good to look at all the dear faces of our family and extended family. We felt overwhelmingly grateful for God's goodness in our lives. Colossians 3:1-2 says, "If then you were raised with Christ, seek those things which are above, where Christ is, sitting at the right hand of God. Set your mind on things above, not on things on the earth." The word *set* implies using discipline to think "half-full" instead of "half-empty." It's not always easy to remember God's goodness. In our humanity, we often have the attitude that good things are our natural right. Remembering God's goodness is a powerful statement of faith in God.

When the children of Israel crossed over the Jordan River, Joshua instructed each of the leaders of the tribes to gather a stone. Using those "stones of remembrance," they built a memorial to God's provision. The story of the first Passover tells us, "When your son asks you in time to come, saying, 'What is this?' that you shall say to him, 'By strength of hand the Lord brought us out of Egypt, out of the house of bondage'" (Exod. 13:14). Stories, special celebrations, and tangible reminders of where we've been and how God has kept us are important for generations to follow.

On our living-room coffee table is an old Swedish Bible that was passed down from Nancie's great-grandparents. She knows very little of those Swedish grandparents, only that they emigrated to the United States and times were very hard for them. But the Bible itself is a stone of remembrance, reminding us of their stubborn faith in God.

We have high on a shelf in our loft an old violin, now forever silent. It belonged to Bill's grandfather William Carmichael (also married to a Nancy). It is a stone of remembrance of the songs he played, of the joys celebrated within a warm family unit. Family pictures, albums, keepsakes—this prayer journal—can remind us of God's goodness to us. On our sofa is a beautiful, soft afghan that Bill's mother knit for us last Christmas. It too is a stone of remembrance—a reminder that she and Bill's father cover all of us with a blanket of prayers.

We have Aunt Hazel's diaries and Nancie's mother's journal. We have our own letters and journals. Even in the losses—or perhaps *especially* in the losses—we celebrate because of the hope we have of being together in heaven. When Nancie's mother died a year and a half ago, all seven children, their spouses, and their children put together a notebook about the exceptional legacy she had left them.

In looking back, we can't ignore the pain or the hard times. They are inevitably a part of every family. Bill's family often recalls some of their most difficult days when they had moved to Colorado and Bill's father had an accident. It was in those very times that God's presence was especially real. In reading some of Nancie's mother's old letters and in learning of her father's early childhood, we see the keeping hand of God on their lives during painful and difficult times of loss and disillusionment.

Celebrating Communion is a time to remember God's goodness in leading us out of the "bondage of the world" and bringing us into new life in Christ. Some of our most memorable times as a family have been when we gathered together to share Communion, remembering God's goodness to us. Nancie remembers sharing Communion with women in prison. They had just sung their favorite song, "Do Lord, O Do Lord, O Do Remember Me." At that moment of celebrating Christ's work on the cross, Nancie had a very real sense that, indeed, God is good. In taking the time to remember God's goodness, we can say with Job, "You will surely forget your trouble, recalling it only as waters gone by. Life will be brighter than noonday, and darkness will become like morning" (Job 11:16-17, NIV).

I pray that my children will remember God's goodness. I pray that as the years go by, they will see that the true source of all good things is the loving hand of God. Help them cherish tangible and intangible reminders of God's goodness.

God's Goodness

R E F L E C T I O N

"If we savor the good times in youth, we can enjoy them again in old age."

Jeanette Oke, *Once upon a Summer*

"It won't be long before you will look back on that up-tight, high-powered, super-charged issue with a whole new outlook. To be quite candid, you may laugh out loud in the future at something you're eating your heart out over today."

Charles Swindoll, *Growing Strong in the Seasons of Life*

"There is a healing power in a selective memory. As humans we cannot forget our sins and hurts, but through forgiveness we can choose not to remember them."

Gary Gulbranson

F A M I L Y   I N T E R A C T I O N

1 Do you have anything that could be considered a stone of remembrance? Use that item to remind each other of God's goodness to your family.

2 Read Isaiah 49:15-16 with your family. Discuss how it makes you feel that God remembers us—that we are inscribed on the palm of His hand. How does that make us feel about remembering Him?

3 Consider tangible ways to celebrate God's goodness to you as a family using special holidays as well as birthdays and anniversaries. For example, on New Year's Eve, spend the hour before midnight sharing something each of you is grateful that God has done in the past year. Put some thought and creativity into your celebrations, making them unique to your family.

4 Read Luke 17:11-19, the story of the ten lepers, only one of whom returned to thank Jesus. Discuss the story. Is it rare to be thankful? What did the spirit of thankfulness do for this man?

C O M M U N I C A T I N G   T H E   B L E S S I N G

I pray for you, my child, that you will remember the good things that God has done for you, the good things you have received. I pray that you will remember these, not the losses or the negative things that have happened. God's peace is ours when we remember His goodness.

MY PRAYER FOR MY CHILD

NAME _____ DATE _____

_____

_____

FOLLOW-UP PRAYERS, ANSWERS, AND INSIGHTS

NAME _____ DATE _____

_____

_____

SEEK WISDOM

46

Wisdom is the principal thing; therefore get wisdom. . . . The fear of the Lord is the beginning of wisdom, and the knowledge of the Holy One is understanding.

Proverbs 4:7; 9:10

PRAYER

Lord, Your Word teaches us that *wisdom* means "knowing God's will and doing it." I don't have much trouble knowing Your will in most things, Lord. It's that "doing it" part that often trips me up. I pray that You will give my child not only the knowledge of what is true and right but also a desire to do it. Give my child insights into Your ways and discernment to see what You want him or her to do. Help my child to study both books and life itself, realizing that You are the source of all wisdom.

"For attaining wisdom and discipline; for understanding words of insight; for acquiring a disciplined and prudent life, doing what is right and just and fair; for giving prudence to the simple, knowledge and discretion to the young—let the wise listen and add to their learning" (Prov. 1:2-5, NIV).

I N S I G H T

Wisdom means understanding what is true, right, and permanent. Watching my mother's death confronted me (Nancie) with my own mortality, and now it seems important that I not waste my life, that I not waste time, that I apply my heart to wisdom.

Days seemed like years as we kept vigil near my mother's bedside, and we children came and went, watching her decline hourly. In those final days, we had some sweet moments, smiles, and even laughter together. But watching her die and trying to make her comfortable as she left us was wrenching. Finally, the struggle was over, and time as she knew it—minutes, days, months, years—stopped. At 4:50 on a Tuesday morning, my sister, who was doing night duty, called me: "Mom's with Jesus."

Just days before, when I'd walked into Mother's room, she had opened her brown eyes with alarm, as she often did after she had been asleep, worried about the time. "What time is it?" she had asked. "I have to get going!" It was an instinctive habit after years

of catching a quick nap on the couch while dinner was cooking. I had helped her to the bathroom one of the last times she was up. Exhausted by the effort of walking, she had sat back on her bed, and I had held her upright. She had leaned into me, a slight smile on her face, content just to be close.

What time is it, Mother? I mused. This is the woman who used to awaken my sisters and me by bursting into our room in the morning, inappropriately cheerful (we thought), quoting, "Dost thou love life? Then do not waste time, for that is the stuff of which life is made!" We girls would groan and roll over.

Mother's words echo in my mind. "I have to get going." Going? I suppose I have to get going, but where? To what? "We finish our years like a sigh. . . . It is soon cut off, and we fly away. . . . So teach us to number our days, that we may gain a heart of wisdom" (Ps. 90:9-12).

Becoming a person of wisdom takes time. It

takes a lot of listening and learning. It's a process of testing, of waiting, of studying. As I look at my mother's life now, I see it as a tapestry, a completed piece of art. There are dark places in the picture, but overall, the dark places add depth and meaning to the portrait of a woman with a quest to know God, with a hunger for His Word. She grew into a woman of wisdom, of gentle graces.

One of Mother's favorite verses was, "A man's days resemble grass. He blossoms like a flower in the field; the wind blows over it, and it is gone, with not a sign that it has ever been there. But the Lord's faithful love rests eternally upon those who revere Him, and His righteousness on the children's children, on those who are faithful to His covenant, who remember to carry out His instructions" (Ps. 103:15-18, Berkeley).

Too often we get in a frenzy—we are frantic to make our lives significant. But Scripture tells us, "Wisdom is the principal thing; therefore get wisdom. And in all your getting, get under-standing" (Prov. 4:7). We build our lives into beautiful places filled with precious and pleas-ant riches by allowing the treasures of God's Word to become an integral, living part of us.

I pray that my children will become seekers of wis-dom. I pray that they will realize that the source of all true wisdom is from above, that the fear of the Lord is the beginning of wisdom. I pray that they will open their hearts to allow God's truth and wisdom deep inside.

R E F L E C T I O N

"May my life be a continual prayer; a long act of love.
May nothing distract me from You, neither noise nor diversions.
O my Master, I would so love to live with You in silence.
But what I love above all is to do Your will,
and since You want me to still remain in the world,
I submit with all my heart for love of You.
I offer you the cell of my heart; may it be Your little Bethany.
Come rest there; I love You so."

Blessed Elizabeth of the Trinity

"Wisdom is the wealth of the wise."

Anonymous

FAMILY INTERACTION

1 Ask your child, "How are you building your house (yourself) with wisdom and understanding?"

2 Spend some time thinking, studying, and praying about wisdom—the principal thing. Ask your child, "How can you pursue wisdom?" Share with your child your response to the same question.

COMMUNICATING THE BLESSING

I pray for you, my child, that you have wisdom. Remember that knowledge is only a step toward wisdom and that the fear of the Lord is the beginning of wisdom.

MY PRAYER FOR MY CHILD

NAME _____ DATE _____

_____

_____

_____

_____

_____

FOLLOW-UP PRAYERS, ANSWERS, AND INSIGHT

NAME _____ DATE _____

_____

_____

_____

_____

LORD, HELP MY CHILD TO BECOME . . .

An Encourager

A Kingdom Builder

A Listener

A Treasure Hunter

A Vow Keeper

A Well Digger

PART 5

LORD, HELP MY CHILD TO BECOME AN . . .

ENCOURAGER

47

A wholesome tongue is a tree of life, but perverseness in it breaks the spirit.

Proverbs 15:4

PRAYER

Lord, what a refreshing gift we can offer one another: encouragement. That is what Your Holy Spirit does for us, Father. You come alongside of us, encouraging us, comforting us, helping us to look forward. I pray that my child will become an encourager to siblings, other family members, friends, and those who are discouraged. Help all of us in the family unit to be encouragers, to replace put-downs with encouragement.

SCRIPTURE

"Encourage one another daily" (Heb. 3:13, NIV).

Encouragement is a rare quality, one that does not come easily to most of us. The meanings of the Greek and Hebrew words for encouragement are "to urge forward, to persuade, to comfort, and to be an advocate." When Moses handed over the reins of leadership to Joshua and the tribal leaders, he encouraged them: "Look, the Lord your God has set the land before you; go up and possess it, as the Lord God of your fathers has spoken to you; do not fear or be discouraged" (Deut. 1:21).

Moses was able to offer encouragement because he had experienced God's grace. He had experienced the miraculous delivery out of Egypt, through the great trials and plagues. The Red Sea parted just in time for the children of Israel to escape Pharaoh's army. Water came from a rock to soothe their thirst. God fed them manna in the wilderness. Moses' words of encouragement were not hollow; they were tried and true.

At its very heart, encouragement is generosity of spirit—offering to someone else the courage to go on, offering someone else the grace that you yourself have received.

Amy, our fourteen-year-old daughter, often leaves little notes on our desks or on a dresser. Bill often finds on his desk a little note

Encourager

from Amy: "I love you." Once when I (Nancie) had to go away for a speaking engagement, I opened my Bible to find a note from her: "Mom, I'm glad you are my mother. God loves you!" As I sat on the platform waiting to speak, her simple note gave me courage to go on. When we offer encouragement, we literally offer life to someone—strength to go on. Encouragement is a wonderful gift, one we must nurture.

Years ago when our children were tiny, we were at a conference where Bill was the speaker. I sat with the children in the back row, trying to keep them in line. That day they were unusually unruly. I was tired, on the verge of tears, and was feeling like a failure as a mother. I was wishing I could be home instead of trying to sit there as if I had it all together. To make matters worse, Bill was speaking about parenting. Just before the meeting started, an elderly pastor sat next to me. "You remind me of my wife when we were young," he said. "She always had to sit alone with the children in church. But let me tell you something." He leaned forward, his eyes bright. "Don't worry about doing everything right, following all the experts. Just love those children. That's what we did, and they turned out great!" He patted me on the shoulder and left, never knowing how his words were *life* to me at that moment.

Proverbs 18:21 says, "Death and life are in the power of the tongue, and those who love it will eat its fruit." Our words have incredible power, especially within the family and among close friends. We can urge someone to "life" by offering encouragement, or we can sentence someone to "death" by uttering negative, harsh words.

Offering encouragement can be very simple. Perhaps all it takes is just a smile, a touch on the shoulder, a sincere "How are you doing?" Offering encouragement can involve taking a moment to write a note to put in your children's lunch bags or a thoughtful card when

they're facing a hurdle. Often in our parenting efforts to correct, discipline, and train, we forget to encourage. We can encourage our children by affirming them when they keep their bedrooms picked up or when they show a better attitude. These gestures of encouragement say, "You're not alone. You can make it!"

I pray that my children will become encouragers, that they will use their words and actions to urge people forward, to comfort them, and to give them the courage to go on. I pray that my children's words will bring life to other people, especially to people who don't know God.

R E F L E C T I O N

"Discouraged people don't need critics. They hurt enough already. They don't need more guilt or piled-on distress. They need encouragement. They need a refuge."

Charles Swindoll, *Growing Strong in the Seasons of Life*

"Life is short, and we have never too much time for gladdening the hearts of those who are traveling the dark journey with us. Oh, be swift to love, make haste to be kind!"

Henri-Frédéric Amiel, *Amiel's Journal*

"It is important to stress that every human being is called upon to be a healer. Although there are many professions asking for special long and arduous training, we can never leave the task of healing to the specialists. We are all healers who can reach out."

Henri Nouwen, *The Wounded Healer*

"You can make more friends in two months by becoming interested in other people than you can in two years by trying to get other people interested in you."

Dale Carnegie

FAMILY INTERACTION

1. In your family discussion time, ask each person to describe how it felt when someone encouraged him or her recently.

2. Ask each family member to talk about a person who is an encourager. What does that person do and say to encourage other people?

3. Talk with your family about people who may need your encouragement. Share specific ideas about how you can encourage them.

4. Talk with your family about whether it is more difficult to encourage someone close to you (family or friends) or to encourage someone you don't know as well.

5. Discuss the effect discouragement has on a person.

COMMUNICATING THE BLESSING

I pray for you, my child, to become a person who learns the secret of being an encourager. How desperately we all need people to encourage us, to urge us on to become the people God wants us to be. I pray that you will know the joy of standing alongside other people, of cheering them on, of giving them the courage to take risks.

MY PRAYER FOR MY CHILD

NAME _____ DATE _____

_____

_____

FOLLOW-UP PRAYERS, ANSWERS, AND INSIGHTS

NAME _____ DATE _____

_____

_____

Encourager

KINGDOM BUILDER

48

Do not fear, little flock, for it is your Father's good pleasure to give you the

kingdom . . . a treasure in the heavens that does not fail, where no thief approaches

nor moth destroys. For where your treasure is, there your heart will be also.

Luke 12:32-34

PRAYER

Lord, many kinds of people are part of Your kingdom. There are the spectators, those who observe, sometimes pass judgment, but never come close. There are the seekers, those who are looking intently but have yet to take the leap of faith. There are the followers, those who find You but who, for a myriad of reasons, stop just inside the door. And then there are the kingdom builders, those who believe in You, surrender themselves to You, and serve You in ways that make an eternal difference. I pray that my child will be a kingdom builder.

"Whoever comes to Me, and hears My sayings and does them, I will show you whom he is like: He is like a man building a house, who dug deep and laid the foundation on the rock. And when the flood arose, the stream beat vehemently against that house, and could not shake it, for it was founded on the rock. But he who heard and did nothing is like a man who built a house on the earth without a foundation, against which the stream beat vehemently; and immediately it fell" (Luke 6:47-49).

Kingdom Builder

Nancie's father was a wheat farmer, a man of the seasons. Her family learned early in life what it meant to plow the soil, sow the seed, and then wait for the harvest. Bill's father was a building contractor, and Bill and his brother and sister learned what it took to construct a building from architectural drawings and plans.

Our parents taught us not only by their vocations but also by their life investments. Our parents were not perfect, but they kept their eyes on the big picture. They were and are kingdom builders. Nancie remembers how several times a week her father would make a point to visit a housebound person, to pray with someone who was ill, to take food or money to someone who needed help. Every Sunday morning without fail, he would teach Sunday school at the local rest home, bringing encouragement and smiles. Nancie's mother taught Sunday school, was a 4-H leader, and maybe most important, poured her life into her seven children, encouraging them in school, in music lessons, and in giving their best to the Lord.

Bill's parents invested their lives in the local church and in their family. Their home was known for its hospitality. As Bill was growing up, he remembers the many people who stayed in his parents' home: missionary families, people in ministry, young people who needed a home for a while. Our parents' children and many of their grandchildren are involved in active ministry, seeking to build the kingdom of God. These life investments have paid rich dividends in the lives of many people.

Being a kingdom builder is not so much doing God's work as it is being God's person. It involves perspective and motivation. It's looking at the big picture and investing in life accordingly. Being a kingdom builder involves understanding that there are seasons:

preparation time, sowing time, waiting time, and then the harvest.

We pray that our children will look beyond their immediate needs and desires to see what results will come from kingdom building. How we long for our children to go after the good stuff—the things that really count for eternity. Sometimes it's hard to remember that kingdom building involves seasons. We most likely will have to wait to see fruit. We must remember that planting God's Word in our children's lives and living an example of a kingdom builder where we are most transparent—our homes— are the most powerful ways to invest in our own families. Remember, "For as the rain comes down, and the snow from heaven, and do not return there, but water the earth, and make it bring forth and bud, that it may give seed to the sower and bread to the eater, so shall My word be that goes forth from My mouth; it shall not return to Me void, but it shall accomplish what I please, and it shall prosper in the thing for which I sent it" (Isa. 55:10-11).

Looking back, I'm sure our parents were not trying to stuff some philosophy down our throats. They simply believed there was no higher calling than to invest in eternity and lived that belief for us to see.

I pray that my children will become kingdom builders, that they will know the deep satisfaction that comes from investing in the gospel of the Lord Jesus Christ. I pray that they will love Him wholeheartedly and live a life of service out of that love.

R E F L E C T I O N

"All that is not eternal is out of date."

C. S. Lewis

"Could I climb to the highest place in Athens, I would lift my voice and proclaim: 'Fellow citizens, why do ye turn and scrape every stone to gather wealth and take so little care of your children, to whom one day you must relinquish it all?'"

Socrates

"The most terrible thing about materialism, even more terrible than its proneness to violence, is its boredom."

Malcolm Muggeridge

FAMILY INTERACTION

1 Read Matthew 6:19-21, 31-34, and discuss the meaning of the verses.

2 Have each family member list three things that would build one's own kingdom and five things that would build God's kingdom.

3 Talk about how your family gives to God's work, why your family tithes, why you spend time in service to God's work. Make a list of how your family can be kingdom builders. Set some reachable goals.

COMMUNICATING THE BLESSING

I pray for you, my child, that you will become a kingdom builder: one who spends energies and uses talents to further God's kingdom.

MY PRAYER FOR MY CHILD

NAME _____ DATE _____

_____

_____

_____

_____

FOLLOW-UP PRAYERS, ANSWERS, AND INSIGHTS

NAME _____ DATE _____

_____

_____

_____

Kingdom Builder

LORD, HELP MY CHILD TO BECOME A . . .

LISTENER

Let every man be swift to hear, slow to speak, slow to wrath.

James 1:19

PRAYER

Lord, what a difficult thing it is to *listen*. I pray, Lord, that my child will learn to listen to You and will know that listening to You is the beginning of wisdom. I pray that my child will use the filter of Your Word to become a true listener so that he or she doesn't listen to the wrong voices. May my child learn that listening involves more than hearing and understanding with the ears; it is hearing and understanding with the heart as well.

SCRIPTURE

"Listen carefully to Me, and eat what is good, and let your soul delight itself in abundance. Incline your ear, and come to Me. Hear, and your soul shall live" (Isa. 55:2-3).

When our son Andy was a sophomore, he had a basketball game that was on the other side of the state, and we weren't able to go this time. The local radio station carried the game live, and we had tuned in at home, even though the reception was terrible. Other frequencies kept breaking in and interfering, making it impossible for us to make sense of the play-by-play account.

At halftime, we grabbed the car keys and said, "Let's go!" As we drove the thirty miles west toward Redmond, where the radio station was based, the reception became clearer. Finally we pulled off the highway, parked under the cold, starry sky, and leaned back, listening for the big moment when Andy would get into the game. Sure enough, with one minute to go, Andy got in and made a three pointer! We jubilantly hugged each other!

As we drove home, we thought about listening. How easy it is to *hear,* but how difficult to *listen.* Things can distract us. Living in a family, we hear a lot, but do we listen to one another? To listen means to respond, to be present to the one who is speaking. At times we parents become tempted to treat our children as commodities—little people put into our care. We can, instead of seeing a real individual, see a face that needs to be washed, homework that needs to be done, chores that

need doing. In our efforts to have good children, it is tempting at times to focus more on their behavior than on *listening* to this wonderful person with unique gifts and talents.

One of the best ways to teach our children to listen is for us to listen to them. Sometimes we need to listen "between the lines" to hear what they are saying to us, to get beneath the obvious. When we feel that someone has listened to us, we are visible. Listening is a most eloquent way to say "I love you."

As a family, we can practice listening for God's voice. Sometimes we listen for God's voice in the wrong places. Discouraged and disheartened, the Old Testament prophet Elijah retreated to the desert and wanted to die. He desperately needed to hear from God. He listened for God in a great wind, but His voice was not there. He listened in an earthquake, but God's voice was not there. He saw a fire pass by, but God did not speak there. Later God spoke to Elijah in an unlikely way—in a gentle whisper, a still, small voice.

Sometimes the static in our lives crackles loudly, and we don't hear God clearly. W. H. Auden wrote, "It is where we are wounded that God speaks to us." We don't like the desert places, the painful places, but we often

Listener

listen best when life is stripped of its distractions, its clamoring interferences. We do amazing things to avoid pain and feelings of inadequacy. But if we allow ourselves to be still in those places and know God there, to listen to what He says to us through His Word, we can become more effective listeners to others.

Real listening takes work. It is not something that comes naturally to most of us. It's costly. It costs me the desire to talk first; it costs me the need to be right; it costs me the desire to have an opinion before fully hearing the evidence. Listening strikes at the heart of who we are. It hits our most basic, selfish instinct— to be first, to be right, to get our own way.

Real listening is not passive; it requires a response. I cannot be lazy and be a good listener. Listening through the layers of conversation to the heart takes effort. It involves openness and selectivity, depth and discernment. Listening involves asking good questions and knowing when to be silent and wait rather than jump ahead in our thoughts, finish sentences for people, or formulate a reply before they're even finished speaking.

Listening to others is a most eloquent way to say "I love you." Jesus said, "Greater love has no one than this, than to lay down one's life for his friends" (John 15:13). Listening is a way to lay down our lives, to lay down our own desires in order to hear and understand the other person. We can love because we know we are loved by the great Listener.

I pray that my children will learn the importance of listening, of being aware of life's real agendas, of learning God's wisdom, and of listening to others. I pray that my children will learn to listen with their hearts as well as their ears. May my children listen for His voice.

R E F L E C T I O N

"He who can no longer listen to his brother will soon be no longer listening to God either, he will be doing nothing but prattle in the presence of God, too. Christians have forgotten that the ministry of listening has been committed to them by Him who is Himself the great listener and whose work they should share."

Dietrich Bonhoeffer

"Listening . . . means taking a vigorous, human interest in what is being told us. You can listen like a blank wall or like a splendid auditorium where every sound comes back fuller and richer."

Alice Duer Miller, *Promises for Parents*

F A M I L Y I N T E R A C T I O N

1 Ask your child, "Whom do you feel really listens to you? How do you feel when someone really listens to you?" Share your responses to the same questions.

2 Ask your child, "Do you feel that I listen to you? If so, what indicates to you that I am listening? What can I do to listen more carefully to you?" Listen carefully.

3 Discuss these questions: How do you feel when someone interrupts you when you are talking? How do you feel when you share an important thought or feeling and the other person doesn't respond at all?

4 Ask your child, "How can we learn to listen to God?" Share your response to the question.

C O M M U N I C A T I N G T H E B L E S S I N G

I pray for you, my child, that you will become a listener. I pray that you will learn to hear God's voice above the noises of everyday life. Learn to listen for God's voice in the right places—His Word, in the direction given by godly adults, and in the still, small voice that speaks in the desert times. I pray that you will also learn to listen to what other people say, not only with their mouths but also with their hearts.

MY PRAYER FOR MY CHILD

NAME _____ DATE _____

_____

_____

FOLLOW-UP PRAYERS, ANSWERS, AND INSIGHTS

NAME _____ DATE _____

_____

_____

Listener

LORD, HELP MY CHILD TO BECOME A . . .

TREASURE HUNTER

50

My heart stands in awe of Your word.

I rejoice at Your word as one who finds great treasure.

Psalm 119:161-162

PRAYER

God, it is exciting to dig for hidden treasure. I pray that my child will love to be a treasure hunter, that he or she will seek to find Your secret treasures. I pray that my child will dig out the good stuff and realize that the most valuable treasures often are not on the surface but are deep in the heart.

SCRIPTURE

"Oh, the depth of the riches both of the wisdom and knowledge of God! How unsearchable are His judgments and His ways past finding out!" (Rom. 11:33).

One of our most enjoyable family traditions is a treasure hunt on Easter Sunday mornings. Nancie hides surprises and clues all over the house. When the kids were younger, they often awakened us early on Easter morning with their delighted cries as they ran up and down the stairs, following the clues to their hidden treasures.

This past summer, we took the vacation of a lifetime. We had saved up our airline bonus miles and surprised our family with a vacation to the Cayman Islands. One of the specialties of the Cayman Islands is diving and snorkeling to see the beautiful tropical fish, exotic sea turtles, and shellfish that live in the crystal-clear water.

Treasure Hunter

One day we chartered a local boat for fishing and snorkeling. Our guide, a specialist at diving for conch, invited us to join in the search for live conch. Conch have beautiful, smooth, pink shells on the inside, but on the outside they look much like the surrounding coral and are difficult to spot. Jon, Eric, Chris, and Andy all joined in the search, but it wasn't three minutes before Andy, the youngest of the four, surfaced with the first conch.

"Lucky!" hollered Eric as he came up empty-handed, spitting salt water. Two minutes later, Andy surfaced with another beautiful conch,

grinning from ear to ear. In about fifteen minutes, Andy had found four conches, and his three brothers had not found a single one. Back in the boat, Andy enjoyed the slaps on the back from all of us as we agreed he somehow had a special knack for finding the treasure we were looking for.

That evening as I (Bill) looked back on the wonderful day, I thanked God for the special memories we had made. I realized that Andy had demonstrated a quality I desired for all of us: the ability to hunt for treasure and recognize it when we see it. I want our children to develop skills for finding spiritual treasures that God has for us. We all see the same terrain, but some people have a special ability to view the terrain and spot God's gems of understanding and insight.

I realized that I can help my children become treasure hunters in two ways. First, I can share with them the treasures I have found. When I see God in the ordinary events of the day, I can share my insight with my children. Second, I can affirm my children when they spot God's treasures. Just as we all congratulated Andy when he found the conches, I can give verbal affirmation when our children find a treasure. When Amy comes home from school and talks about how she felt pained when a child was belittled at school, I can say, "Amy, what you experienced in your heart today was God's compassion for that child. That's a real treasure." Or when Chris tells us that he has decided to trust God with a major decision he has to make, I can say, "Chris, you have discovered a wonderful treasure: When we trust God to guide us, He will lead us in the right direction. I'm so glad you are searching for His best for you."

When we practice looking for God's presence around us, we see His hand every-where. We must continue to look for His treasure, even when circumstances over-whelm us. When we are determined to search, we will find His peace in the midst of the storm.

I pray that my children will become treasure hunters, that they will eagerly hunt for the treasures God has hidden for us in secret places. I pray that my children will have the persistence and fortitude to mine the deep places of God's Word and their own hearts to find life's true riches.

R E F L E C T I O N

"Find out, then, where your treasure really is. Discern substance from accident.
Don't confuse your meals with your life and your clothes with your body.
Don't lose your head over what perishes. . . . Accumulating things is useless. . . .
The fewer the things and the people you 'simply must have'
the nearer you will be to the idea of happiness."

Evelyn Underhill, *House of the Soul*

"If a child is to keep alive his inborn sense of wonder, he needs the companionship
of at least one adult who can share it, rediscovering with him the joy,
excitement, and mystery of the world we live in."

Rachel Carson, *The Sense of Wonder*

"Our treasure may of course be small and inconspicuous, but its size is immaterial;
it all depends on the heart, on ourselves. And if we ask how we are to know where
our hearts are, the answer is just as simple—everything which hinders us from loving
God above all things and acts as a barrier between ourselves and our obedience
to Jesus is our treasure, and the place where our heart is."

Dietrich Bonhoeffer, *The Cost of Discipleship*

FAMILY INTERACTION

1 Ask each family member to answer this question: "If you had fifteen minutes to evacuate your home, what would you take with you? Why are these things important to you?"

2 Ask each family member to discuss a time when he or she was searching for something valuable. Answer these questions: "What were you looking for (a gift for someone, a solution to a problem, a person to help you do something, a person with certain characteristics, etc.)? What did you do to search for that treasure? Why was it important for you to find it?"

3 What are God's unfathomable riches, and how do we seek them? Read Matthew 6:20-21.

COMMUNICATING THE BLESSING

I pray for you, my child, that you will be a treasure hunter, seeking the unfathomable riches of God. Follow Him wherever He may take you, finding riches more precious than silver or gold. I pray that you also will look for the treasures God has hidden in your own heart: love, joy, peace, patience, kindness, goodness, faithfulness, gentleness, and self-control. When you find these treasures, I pray that you will share them with others.

MY PRAYER FOR MY CHILD

NAME _____ DATE _____

_____

_____

_____

FOLLOW-UP PRAYERS, ANSWERS, AND INSIGHTS

NAME _____ DATE _____

_____

_____

LORD, HELP MY CHILD TO BECOME A . . .

Vow Keeper

51

For you, O God, have heard my vows; You have given me the heritage

of those who fear Your name. . . . So I will sing praise to Your name forever,

that I may daily perform my vows.

Psalm 61:5, 8

P R A Y E R

Lord, I pray that my child will be a person who keeps promises. Unkept vows fill our culture with broken hearts, bitterness, and spiritual bankruptcy. Help my child to make commitments that he or she is willing to keep, even at personal inconvenience and sacrifice.

S C R I P T U R E

"Here am I, and the children the Lord has given me. We are signs and symbols in Israel from the Lord Almighty" (Isa. 8:18, NIV).

In her book *Traits of Healthy Families,* Dorothy Curran noted that families that seem to survive well in this culture are ones that know how to celebrate. It's especially important to celebrate the vows that we make at confirmations, weddings, and anniversaries. Celebrating our promises is important because the vows that we make give our lives their definition and shape.

Bill and I have made several vows during our lives: to follow Christ, to marry each other, to parent the children God has given us, to be faithful to our work and callings.

When we make vows or promises, we give the gift of ourselves. Keeping these vows shows more than anything else what we really believe. How we live out our vows speaks to our children about things that are good and essential, things worth preserving.

Not long ago, Bill and I witnessed our first-born son stand at an altar and make a vow to Brittni Estep to love her, cherish her, and honor her as long as they both live. Then we witnessed Brittni's vows to Jon. A few short years ago, we celebrated our twenty-fifth wedding anniversary, remembering the promises we had made to each other.

Historian Arnold Toynbee observed, "Civilizations which relinquished their commitment to core values lost their moral vision and have not survived." How do we who are weak and frail—we who often cannot keep our promises—dare make these commitments?

We keep our vows by being present to them—fully conscious, fully choosing. We can be in a marriage, yet not *be there.* We can be a parent, yet not *be there* for our child. Listen to Jesus' promises to us: "I am with you until the end of the earth." "I will never leave you or forsake you." "I will come again." We dare to make vows because Jesus keeps His promises to us. There is a God-shaped vacuum in all of us—holy ground. Henri Nouwen wrote, "Marriage . . . is an intimacy that is based on the common participation in a love greater than the love two people can offer each other." We dare to make vows because we know this greater love—the "Love that does not let us go."

Let's face it, Hallmark doesn't make cards for some occasions. Sometimes we don't feel like celebrating our marriages or celebrating being a parent. We may give it all we've got, and it's not good enough. The reality of it is that nourishing our promises and keeping those vows means sticking with it in the ordinary times, the tedious times, the boring times. It means doing the right thing even if there's nothing in it for me. It means believing in our callings, being faithful, trying again to teach Scripture to our children in innovative, fresh ways.

A vow is not really a vow until it's tested. Often we're afraid of the testing. And yet that is the very place where God proves Himself to us. Both Bill and I can look back not only at our parents' walk with God but also at our own and see how we were tested in hard times, how God proved Himself true. The triumphs were not achieved in one single blinding moment.

It was in the daily walk. "You have tested my heart; You have visited me in the night; You have tried me and have found nothing. I have purposed that my mouth shall not transgress. . . . By the word of Your lips, I have kept away from the paths of the destroyer. Uphold my steps in Your paths, that my footsteps may not slip" (Ps. 17:3-5). God's mercies hold us when our vows are being tested and purified.

I pray that my children will have the courage to give themselves to God and know that He is the love that will never let them go. And in the security of that love, may my children learn to keep their life promises, the covenants that shape their lives.

R E F L E C T I O N

"Covenant, when fulfilled in trust, will enable us to survive tensions, resolve differences, and grow together beyond cultural diversity. . . . Covenant is the highest form of commitment that engages the human spirit. Trust is built on the reality of covenant."

Myron and Esther Augsburger, *How to Be a Christ-Shaped Family*

"I do wish our young people understood that the marriage vows are intended as a lifetime commitment and that's the way it works best."

James Dobson, *Turn Your Heart toward Home*

"Consider the postage stamp. Its usefulness lies in its ability to stick to one thing until it gets there."

Anonymous

FAMILY INTERACTION

1 As a family, discuss the important vows you've made and the ways in which you are living them out.

2 Over a period of time, read Daniel 1–6 together with your child. Ask your child, "What were the vows that Daniel and the Hebrew young men made? How did those vows impact their lives?"

3 Ask your child, "What is the most important thing you have promised to do? How are you doing in keeping that promise?"

4 Discuss with your child the foolishness of making promises or vows that cannot be kept.

COMMUNICATING THE BLESSING

I pray for you, my child, that you will be a person of your word, never to make vows lightly or without solemn deliberation. I pray that once you give your word or make your vow that you will do whatever is necessary to see that you keep it.

MY PRAYER FOR MY CHILD

NAME _____ DATE _____

_____

_____

_____

FOLLOW-UP PRAYERS, ANSWERS, AND INSIGHTS

NAME _____ DATE _____

_____

_____

_____

LORD, HELP MY CHILD TO BECOME A . . .

WELL DIGGER

52

And Isaac dug again the wells of water which they had dug

in the days of Abraham his father.

Genesis 26:18

P R A Y E R

Lord, how grateful I am for Your well of living water that so deeply satisfies my thirst for life's meaning. How You sustain me, refresh me, keep me growing. Father, I pray that my child will see the need to dig out his or her own wells, to search for You with diligence. As a parent, I can't dig my child's wells; my child must dig them himself or herself. I pray that my example of my own quest for You may inspire my child to see that You, indeed, are my wellspring.

S C R I P T U R E

"Choose for yourselves this day whom you will serve. . . . But as for me and my house, we will serve the Lord" (Josh. 24:15).

Not long ago *Christian Parenting Today* did a survey to see what worried parents the most. One response we heard was typical of many: "I'm afraid my child will not follow God." How amazing (and sometimes disconcerting to us parents) that God respects us enough to give us a free will. One of the most difficult things Christian parents face is relinquishing their child to God, knowing that "God has no grandchildren, only children." Each of us must come to God on our own. Just as Isaac had to dig out the wells that his father had dug many years earlier, so our children need to choose to follow God as we did many years ago.

Well Digger

We know God deals with us individually, but sometimes we are tempted to wish our children could just slide into God's kingdom on our coattails and be spared the struggle. But if we look back through time, we see a record of *individuals* and their God. Parents can set godly examples, whet their children's appetites for the things of God. But throughout Scripture, the quest to know God is a solitary one.

"Work out your own salvation with fear and trembling," Paul admonished in Philippians 2:12. It's not that we earn salvation, negating Christ's work of grace on the cross. But we are like Jacob: At some time in our lives, we must meet God one-on-one.

The wonderful thing we see in God's dealing with us is how patient He is. He longs to establish a relationship, and when we do find Him, He deals with us uniquely. How important it is that our children see the need to dig out their own wells, to search for Him with all their hearts.

Isaac knew where his father's wells were located, but it was up to him to dig out the dirt that had plugged up the well. He had to dig it out to get to the water. Our children can see where the wells are, but if they want to drink personally and deeply from those wells, they must dig out the truths of God and pursue Him on their own.

As a young mother, I (Nancie) was often unable to get to the women's Bible study on a regular basis since I had two small toddlers and an infant. I remember thinking one morning, *There's nothing stopping me from reading the Bible on my own.* I thought back to my first memories of my mother: Every morning she was absorbed in reading God's Word as if it were life itself. She never told me in so many words, "Nancie, you need to read the Bible every day because it's important." But I saw through her life her source of Living Water. I knew where the water was. It was up to me, however, to dig down deep for myself. And I have never been disappointed!

As parents, we cannot dig out the wells for our children, but we can make sure our own well is flowing freely, and we can pray that the example of our own quest may inspire our children to remember that He is their source.

I pray that my children will thirst for the living water, knowing that when they drink it, they will never again be satisfied with anything less. I pray that my children's desire to grow deeply in the things of God will increase as they begin a lifelong pursuit of God.

R E F L E C T I O N

"If we could see beneath the surface of many a life, we would see that thousands of people within the Church are suffering spiritually from 'arrested development'; they never reach spiritual maturity; they never do all the good they were intended to do; and this is due to the fact that at some point in their lives they refused to go further; some act of self-sacrifice was required of them, and they felt they could not and would not make it; some habits had to be given up, some personal relation altered and renounced, and they refused to take the one step which would have opened up for them a new and vital development."

Olive Wyon

"Once while traveling in a sandy region I was tired and thirsty. Standing on the top of a mound I looked for water. The sight of a lake at a distance brought joy to me, for now I hoped to quench my thirst. I walked toward it for a long time, but I could never reach it. Afterward I found out that it was a mirage, only a mere appearance of water. In like manner I was moving about the world in search of the water of life. The things of this world—wealth, position, honor, and luxury— looked like a lake by drinking of whose waters I hoped to quench my spiritual thirst."

Sadhu Sundar Singh

"I think that God wants each of his children to be a sort of artesian well."

Dwight L. Moody

FAMILY INTERACTION

1 As a family, read Genesis 24–35 over a period of time. As you read, discuss the various ways God dealt with Abraham and Isaac (chapter 24), Esau and Jacob (chapter 25), Isaac (chapter 26), Jacob and Esau (chapters 27–29), Rachel and Leah (chapter 30), etc. Retell the stories in your own words, and elicit responses from different family members.

2 After discussing each story, ask your child, "What can we learn from this person's life?"

3 Tell your family about a specific time when you personally confronted God. Perhaps it was the time you first asked for forgiveness from sin; perhaps a time when you realized it was up to you to make Him Lord of your life.

COMMUNICATING THE BLESSING

I pray for you, my child, that you will dig down deep for yourself to find Jesus, the Living Water. Only He can answer your soul's deepest longings. As wonderful as it is to have a Christian family and heritage, remember that God has no grandchildren—only children—and that you must seek Him for yourself. He has a wonderful, unique plan just for you.

MY PRAYER FOR MY CHILD

NAME _____ DATE _____

_____

_____

FOLLOW-UP PRAYERS, ANSWERS, AND INSIGHTS

NAME _____ DATE _____

_____

_____

Well Digger